THE ROUGH AND ROWDY DEVOTIONAL

FINDING GOD IN 50 FAMILY TALES

KRISTEN JOY WILKS

CONTENTS

Dedication   1

Introduction   2

Part One

1. Riding the Wild Burro   7

2. Fast Gun   11

3. Horse Rustlers   15

4. Riding On Her Own   19

5. Racing the Plow Horses   23

6. Drama With Topsy   27

7. The Empty Gun   31

8. Hunting Turkey and Getting a Bear   35

9. The Hidden Still   39

10. Bouncing Behind a Horse   43

11. Nellie and the Jackrabbit Hunt   47

12. A Fancy Dress and a Broken Leg   51

13. Old Timey Festivities   55

14. Stallion Trouble   59

15. Those Pesky Pranks   63

16. Will You Shoot Against My Girls?   67

17. Fancy Doodads   71

18. Pudgy the Hunting Dog   75

Part 2

19. The Rowdy Suitor   81

20. The Big Move   85

21. The Man Who Lived in a Stump   89

22. Playing Coyote and Hunter   93

23. Cold Winter Nights   96

24. Grandpa Del Gets Autumn Flowers   100

Part 3

25. Forty-two Below Zero with a Handsaw   108

26. A Pack Rat Finds a Way   112

27. Sundance and the Chickens   115

28. Pride Goeth Before the Crash   119

29. Bluff Charged   122

30. The Horse Who Loved Sledding   126

31. Breaking Trail with Captain   130

32. Sundance and the Trees   133

33. The Horse Thief   136

34. Foolishness and a Danger to All   140

35. The Cat Named Stupid   144

Part 4

36. Diving Under the Dock   149

37. The Giant Bouncy Wheel   152

38. Stubbs Goes Waterskiing   156

39. Stubbs Sniffs Out Danger   160

40. Stubbs and the Scattered Bunnies   164

41. Greg and the Ugly Baby   167

Part 5

42. The Dare to Dare   173

43. Praying for a Pony Against my Parents' Wishes   176

44. Dangled Over the Snake Pit   180

45. Sundance and the Scary Bush   184

46. Kristen's Hasty Gallop   188

47. Blind to the Cougar in the Road   192

48. The Wrong Miracle   196

49. A Dust Storm, the Dasher, and a Grumpy   200
     Granny

50. As Brave as a Chicken   204

Rosa's Sourdough Cinnamon Rolls   208

About the author   212

Also by Kristen Joy Wilks   214

To Grandma Autumn . . .

While Del built a Bible camp and a log home in wild country that had previously seen nothing but dark forests, lush meadows, and a ramshackle horse corral, you turned all that you touched into a home. You enfolded our family into your arms when we didn't have a place to live. You bought sugary cereal we couldn't afford and offered your TV for Saturday morning cartoons. When my brother and I played in the deep snow out in front of the house on cold winter afternoons, you called us inside with cups of cocoa made with cream and homemade cinnamon rolls. You sang us the Irish lullaby your mother taught you before she passed and though you started keeping house when you were just a girl, I have never seen anyone more worthy of the title of hostess. Hospitality was your gift and a blessing to everyone you met. You served dinner on china plates and innumerable servings of sugar-filled tea in beautiful china cups to my three obstreperous sons. If one broke, your response was always the same. "They were made to be used." I will always cherish the moments I sat at your 100-year-old oak table with a cup of tea in a fancy cup listening to you tell stories to everyone you loved, especially my pack of rowdy boys. I love you, Grammy. And if the Lord allows you a glimpse of where we've taken the tales you left us to tell, I pray that they will make you proud. We are all trying to learn how to bless others a fraction of the amount that you blessed each of us.

INTRODUCTION

I come from a family of storytellers. Not writers, story-tellers. First came my great grandfather Ben. After working as a U.S. Marshal hunting down outlaws in Oklahoma Territory, a general fast gun, and jack of all trades, Ben found employment telling ghost stories at a dude ranch for wide-eyed city folk. Then my Grandma Autumn welcomed anyone and everyone into her cozy log home with a cup of cocoa and a slice of homemade pie. But that pie wasn't the only sweet treat she offered. Autumn told us stories about horses who went sledding, the dangers of riding a wild burro, and how folks used to use dynamite to celebrate the 4th of July. Grandpa Del would often pipe up with a twinkle in his eye and the tale about that time he and his brother played "Coyote and Hunter" with a real slingshot. On long car rides, my mother Judy kept boredom at bay with stories about her pony having a surprise foal or how they tied a rope around her ankle on camping trips because she sleepwalked. Finally, some of my best childhood memories were of my dad Greg as he sat on the end of my bed telling tales about bouncing a giant wagon wheel down from The Butte at Lake Chelan or made up one of his own Green Meadow Rescue Society stories to ease my earaches as I fell asleep. I have recently learned that a childhood filled with amazing storytellers is a rare and beautiful thing. It only makes sense that when I was asked to write a devotional, I would fall back on the abundant collection of wild tales I grew up hearing. So many different things can point to God, even rough and rowdy family stories. May the Lord meet you on the page as you take a walk through my family lore and are reminded that even the craziest story can reveal the depths of Jesus' love.

PART ONE

AUTUMN'S STORIES

Autumn Maurita Harmon was my paternal grandmother and the daughter of fast shooting Ben Harmon and fancy Texas lady Georgia McFadden. Autumn was the original strong and capable woman in my life. Burnished auburn hair, fancy hats, and homecooked meals were just as much her signature as riding fast horses, spending a winter in a homesteading cabin at forty degrees below zero, and chasing squirrels out of the house with a broom. These devotions are based on the stories Autumn told me. Some include tales about her sisters, brothers, and parents as well. Grab a piece of pie, my friend. Sit back and let Autumn tell you a tale.

1

RIDING THE WILD BURRO

"And if you do not carry your own cross and follow me, you cannot be my disciple. But don't begin until you count the cost. For who would begin construction of a building without first calculating the cost to see if there is enough money to finish it?"

Luke 14:27-28

When my grandma Autumn was a girl, she and her brother Wiley lived in a part of Arizona that was full of wild burros. They were frisky, fun, and adorable.

Those little donkeys looked like the kind of critter a feisty young girl should be riding.

So, Autumn climbed a towering tree and shimmied out onto a big branch that hung over the path. She lay flat so the burros wouldn't notice.

Wiley kicked his horse into a trot and shooed the nearest herd under Autumn's tree.

The burros were trotting beneath her while Autumn gripped her branch waiting for the right moment. As the last burro clip clopped under her tree, she rolled off the branch and landed smack on that burro's back.

These were wild burros. Very wild.

They had never worn a halter, eaten a carrot out of someone's hand, or felt a saddle. That burro had certainly never had a girl swoop out of the sky and land on him.

The burro squealed and exploded into action.

He brayed and bucked and turned in a crazy circle to the right.

Autumn held on but was sliding left. She decided to let go and slide off. Only, the burro changed directions.

The wild burro spun to the left, bucking and braying all the while. Maybe she could slip off his right side?

Nope, the burro spun to the right, once more.

Autumn would do about anything to end her adventure. But as she bounced on that fuzzy critter's back, she looked down at his sharp little hooves.

Would the burro trample her like a rattlesnake if she leaped free?

Up on the hillside, safe on his horse, Wiley was doubled over with laughter.

Finally, that burro spun and bucked close to a fence. There was a short space between the ground and the lowest rail.

Could Autumn make it under in time to escape the beast's hooves?

Wiley wasn't any help, so Autumn took action. As the burro spun and squealed, she flung herself off his back and rolled under the fence.

With no girl on his back or by his hooves, the burro gave a sigh of relief and galloped off to catch the herd.

Neither Autumn nor Wiley ever rode a wild burro again.

Have you ever gotten into a situation that was more than you could handle? Have you ever wished you had thought more about what might happen before taking action?

Jesus tells us to count the cost beforehand. Following Him can be hard. He doesn't want us to be surprised by difficult times but to trust in his love. Sometimes when you count the cost, you realize it's not worth the pain. Like riding a wild burro! But when we see how much God loves us and that following him is full of blessings as well as tough times, we can know it is worth the cost.

Dear Lord,

Help me to learn to count the cost before I act and to avoid dangerous situations. Help me to be thoughtful about following you as well. To know that there will be troubles but to also trust your love. Give me strength from you and the ability to avoid the wild burros along the way.

Amen.

2

FAST GUN

"If I could speak all the languages of earth and of angels, but didn't love others, I would only be a noisy gong or a clanging cymbal."

I Corinthians 13:1

Grandma Autumn's dad was a fast gun.

As a boy, Ben and his friends would lope their horses past a tree while shooting, trying to carve their initials in the trunk before riding past. He could actually do it, too.

Her brother Wiley once saw their dad throw a knife and hit the head of a nail. This wasn't something he did often, though, since it broke the tip off the end of his knife. Ben was so skilled with a gun that he worked as a marshal when he was only eighteen years old. When he hunted wild turkeys, Ben didn't use buckshot. His aim was so good, he'd just shoot their heads right off.

When Autumn was a little girl, they went hiking and she saw him quickdraw and shoot down the path. When they got to that spot in the trail, there was a rattlesnake with its head shot clean off.

Ben once bet a man that he could shoot a hole in his hat even if he put the hat behind a boulder. His friend had a new hat and all his buddies thought it looked really funny since it was so clean and stiff. Not the kind of hat a rancher should have. That hat needed a hole.

Well, the man took him up on the bet because he couldn't see how Ben could possibly shoot the hat with it sitting behind a boulder. Just to be sure, he crammed it down real hard, wedged between some little rocks.

Well, Ben hadn't mentioned that there were some other rocks situated around that boulder. Those rocks sat at just the right angle. He ricocheted the bullet off of a rock to the side and it bounced behind the boulder and hit the hat. Only, Ben's friend ended up with several holes in his hat because the bullet shattered.

Some folks have incredible skills. Skills that baffle the mind. It amazes me that God can make people who can achieve so many amazing things.

But as astounding as humankind can be, if we do not have love, all that we gain loses its luster. Our joy fades and even our accomplishments taste sour.

It is love in the face of hate that is a true achievement. It is living a life of giving instead of taking. I saw this from my grandmother. Autumn was a fair shot with a gun, but that wasn't what impressed. She was the main cook and housekeeper in her home at the age of ten, and she didn't quit until she couldn't walk anymore. She loved those around her with depth and sincerity for ninety-four years. Even chair-bound, she would offer anyone who visited a cup of tea. Now that is amazing. A humble life, lived in love.

Dear Lord,

It would be wonderful to have an amazing skill, to be really good at something, to have people notice when I do a good job. But even if this doesn't happen, please help me to remember that you made me incredibly valuable. I'm a person your son died for. I can do the impossible, love like Jesus. Help me to rest in your love and trust that you can help me to do great things. Not like shooting hidden hats and rattlesnakes, but like offering cocoa to a guest on a cold day and listening and loving like you.

Amen.

3

HORSE RUSTLERS

But now, O Jacob, listen to the LORD who created you. O Israel, the one who formed you says, "Do not be afraid, for I have ransomed you. I have called you by name; you are mine.
Isaiah 43:1

Back in the 1920s, Grandma Autumn's dad, Ben, had to rescue his horse, Tony, from rustlers. Tony was an incredibly special horse. He could do a variety of tricks, including counting. Tony would paw the ground three times when Ben said, "Count to three, Tony" and so on for several different numbers. Tony even came when you called his name. It was this last skill that saved Tony's life when the horse rustlers came through.

Now, just after World War I, horse rustlers weren't just stealing horses to sell to a different owner who would then treat them well. No siree, folks could get money for horse meat that was being sent to feed people in post-war Germany who were starving. The plight of war-torn Germany was terrible, but the horse rustlers were less concerned about hungry people and more concerned about earning a quick and easy buck. They would round up wild horses to sell for meat. They would even round up horses that had brands on them and clearly belonged to someone else.

One day, Autumn's folks were startled to see rustlers ride through their property. They asked to use the corral to sort out which horses they wanted. These men didn't say they were rustlers, but Ben figured it out since they had his horse, Tony, mixed in with their herd.

Her mother, Georgia, hid behind a large boulder with a rifle, waiting to see what would happen. Ben said they could use the corral, but he wanted his horse back. The rustlers had cropped Tony's tail and mane to disguise him, but Autumn's dad would have recognized him anywhere.

It was clear that Tony was his when Ben opened the gate and said, "Tony, let's go to the barn." Tony trotted out of the herd of stolen horses, shook his cropped mane, and followed Ben to the barn. Since Tony knew his name, the rustlers didn't argue.

Just like Ben recognized Tony immediately, even with the ragged haircut, God sees you and he knows you. Even more than Ben and Georgia loved Tony and were willing to fight to keep him safe, God loves you and wants you safe and sound in Heaven with him.

You are seen. You are wanted. The one who loved you enough to die for you is calling you by name. Please don't stay with the herd of stolen horses. Follow the one who loves you and is willing to risk a showdown with rustlers to bring you home.

Dear Lord,

Sometimes I feel like no one sees and knows the real me. Please help me to remember that you created me, you ransomed me, you have called me by name, and I am yours.

When I am afraid, help me to seek you, follow you, and trust in your love.

Amen.

4

RIDING ON HER OWN

"So don't let anyone condemn you for what you eat or drink, or for not celebrating certain holy days or new moon ceremonies or Sabbaths ... You have died with Christ, and he has set you free from the spiritual powers of this world. So why do you keep on following the rules of the world, such as, 'Don't handle! Don't taste! Don't touch!'?"

Colossians 2:16, 20-21

Grandma Autumn started riding by herself at the age of five. Not only did she ride, she rode a big plow horse named Flossie, bareback.

You might imagine a five-year-old couldn't even get onto a plow horse much less ride such a large animal. Well, you would be half right. Autumn couldn't mount her horse, not in the normal way, but just because an adult would have needed a mounting block to get onto Flossie didn't mean that Autumn was deterred.

When Autumn wanted to ride, she would find Flossie wherever she was grazing. Then she would wait. When Flossie reached down for a bite of grass, Autumn quickly swung her leg over the mare's head and sat on her neck, just behind her ears. Then, as Flossie raised her head to chew, Autumn would slide backwards down the mare's neck and onto her back. Finally situated properly, Autumn would give Flossie a kick and off they'd go.

One time, Autumn saw a different horse grazing. Someone else's horse. A horse that she would love to ride. So, full of confidence, Autumn swaggered up to that stranger's horse.

Autumn swung her leg over the animal's head and sat down on his neck, just behind his ears.

The strange horse didn't raise his head, but he did raise his hind end. He bucked and kicked in a rowdy circle. Full of indignation and horsey rage.

Now, Autumn was stuck, right behind his ears with no safe way to get off!

When Autumn was finally able to jump free, she was happy to go back to riding Flossie, her faithful plow horse.

Most people would look at a tiny, five-year-old girl and judge that she couldn't possibly ride a plow horse by herself. They might laugh if you told them that five-year-old Autumn could even mount that huge animal all by herself. But Autumn had a completely new way of doing things.

When Jesus came to live among us, he baffled the Jewish teachers. There were rules for following God. Don't eat pig meat. Don't touch someone with leprosy. Don't do work on a Sabbath day. Jesus provided a completely new way to follow and belong to God. Jesus told his disciple Peter that he could eat whatever his host set before him. Not only did Jesus touch lepers, He healed them of their illness. In fact, he healed them on a Sabbath day!

Just like those who figured that Autumn couldn't mount and ride a huge plow horse by herself were wrong, those who think that following all the rules will make someone a child of God are also wrong. Jesus provided a way to belong to God. A way that depends on his love and sacrifice and not on us at all.

Dear Lord,

Please help me not to be weighed down by all the things I am trying to do just right. Remind me when life gets too heavy, it is not a list of things to do that makes me your child. Remind me of the freedom that Jesus brings. Remind me that I am yours because Jesus died for me and I choose to trust in his sacrifice and his love.

Amen.

5

RACING THE PLOW HORSES

"About that time the disciples came to Jesus and asked,
'Who is greatest in the Kingdom of Heaven?'"
Matthew 18:1

W hen my grandma Autumn was a little girl, she and
her brother Wiley wanted to race horses! Who
wouldn't? However, they didn't own a race horse. They
didn't own any horses at all. Their dad had several horses,
though. The problem. The horses they could ride were his

plow horses, a big white mare named Mabel and a big gray mare named Flossie.

Plow horses were supposed to . . . plow. Not race. However, Autumn and Wiley decided to give it a try. Wiley hopped up onto Mabel and Autumn swung a leg over Flossie's neck and slid onto the gray mare's back when she raised her head after taking a bite of grass. The two children snuck away with the plow horses and then urged them into a lumbering gallop.

And you know what?

They loved it! Flossie and Mabel took to racing like they were born to thunder over the plains, their massive hooves pounding out a rhythm as they ran. Soon both horses didn't just race because the children urged them to. Those horses both wanted to win!

Well, the time came to plow the fields in straight and even rows. Autumn's dad, Ben, hitched up his big, steady plow horses . . . and off they went! Mable would pull ahead and then Flossie would yank her nose forward and get in front of her. Not much plowing happened because the horses were so distracted trying to see who was fastest, they didn't pull the plow together in straight and even rows.

Ben knew exactly what had happened. Nothing made a team of horses forget how to work together like being raced. Nothing kept plow horses from making straight and even rows like wondering which of them was fastest.

Jesus's disciples also had trouble working together. They wanted to know who was first in God's kingdom, who was the greatest of them all. But Jesus knew that there is a greater kind of strength than winning a race.

"So anyone who becomes as humble as this little child is the greatest in the Kingdom of Heaven."

Matthew 18:4

Jesus didn't come to conquer the world with swords and bloodshed and mighty battles. The Son of God himself came to earth as a baby, the unnoticed child of an unwed mother and a simple woodworker. He taught lessons about God to huge crowds but urged those he healed to tell no one of the miracles he performed. In quiet wilderness places, he explained how the last would be first in the kingdom of God.

For what can conquer hard hearts more quickly than a gentle word and forgiving eyes?

Jesus showed us that God's power works in us all the brighter when we love and serve in simple ways. Like two gentle plow horses, pulling their burden together, not worrying about who will come out first.

Dear Lord,

When I want to be first, best, or strongest, please help me to remember what you say is important. Serving others instead of making others do what I want. Showing love and care in your name. Grow me to be like you.

Amen.

6

DRAMA WITH TOPSY

"So where does this leave the philosophers, the scholars, and the world's brilliant debaters? God has made the wisdom of this world look foolish."
I Corinthians 1:20

While Grandma Autumn loved riding the plow horses, it was an incredible day when she got a horse of her own. When her dad bought a ranch, the former owner threw in Topsy to sweeten the deal. Topsy was either a large pony or a small saddle horse and at the tender age of six, Autumn absolutely loved to ride her bareback.

Autumn had recently been to the movies and seen a heroine on horseback who was quite inspiring. This actress had ridden her horse up to the top of a tall knoll and surveyed the valley below in a dramatic fashion. Then, the beautiful heroine had spurred her horse and they had plunged down the knoll into the valley below at a swift, and of course dramatic, speed.

Autumn felt that she and Topsy's drama-filled moment had come.

She rode her new horse up to the top of a tall knoll. Autumn then surveyed the land below, dramatically. Only, Topsy didn't understand. Topsy decided that a little nibble of grass, non-dramatic grass, was in order. She had just settled in for a nice snack when Autumn felt that they had surveyed the land long enough.

Autumn didn't have spurs but decided to give Topsy a nice invigorating whap on the belly with her reins.

Topsy did indeed plunge dramatically into the valley below and at a breakneck speed, to boot. The only problem, she did so without Autumn.

Topsey bolted with so much drama that she ran right out from under Autumn and left my grandmother sitting, all alone, on top of the knoll staring down into the valley after her runaway horse.

In 1 Corinthians, the apostle Paul tells us that even the plans of the most brilliant minds can be shown as foolish by the wisdom of God. The movie heroine's plan to pause and survey the land and then gallop down the hill looked like a brilliant idea to young Autumn. However, copying that cinematic moment proved more painful and embarrassing than what the movie portrayed.

God's way of loving your enemies, doing good in the face of bad things done to you, taking the humble place at the table instead of seeking the top spot, and forgiving with the same extravagance that God forgives us can seem foolish. But the entire world was changed when a single man (you guessed it, Jesus) lived these values out and taught others to do likewise. Autumn would later go on to become the finest hostess I have ever met. Graciously, quietly, she invited anyone and everyone into their log home in the mountains in such a genuine way that people always felt at home. While that dramatic ride into the valley looked like the best plan, Autumn glorified God in another way. She turned their remote, mountain home into a haven. A cup of tea on a cold day and homemade cinnamon toast, with laughter and stories told beside a roaring fire. Autumn was a heroine worthy of admiration, but not because of her fancy ride on Topsy!

Dear Lord,

When I look around and feel small, when everyone else's accomplishments feel huge next to my humble efforts, please remind me of your kind of wisdom. Help me to seek what is great in your kingdom and not worry about what the world thinks is wise.

Amen.

7

THE EMPTY GUN

"Just as damaging as a madman shooting a deadly weapon
is someone who lies to a friend
and then says, 'I was only joking.'"
Proverbs 26:18-19

Grandma Autumn's brother Jack and his cousin Maran were fast friends and enjoyed many adventures together. Not every adventure was smart . . . or safe. When they were teenagers, old enough to know better, they decided to practice their quick draw skills.

Now, they were not lawmen protecting a town or bank robbers causing mayhem, they were teen boys who wanted to shoot fast, just because. In order to develop their fast draw abilities, they decided to practice. Did Jack and Maran practice with toy guns? Nope.

They each owned handguns, which were important tools around the ranch. So, Jack and Maran decided to be careful. They unloaded their guns. With guns unloaded and holstered, the two teens went about their daily chores, but were ready to respond to any pretend attacks. If Jack spotted Maran, he'd jump around the barn and shout, "Draw!" Both boys would draw their guns and pretend to shoot. If Maran saw Jack working in the garden, he'd jump out from behind the milkhouse and shout, "Draw!" The goal was to be so fast on the draw, that they could beat the other at pulling their gun from its holster.

Can you think of any ways that Jack and Maran's game could go awry?

Now, Jack and Maran did this so often and for so long that their reflexes became very quick indeed. Not only were they fast, but by repeating the game over and over, they developed muscle memory that helped them draw automatically whenever they saw the other boy or heard a shouted, "Draw!"

A gun is a tool and eventually Jack needed to use his for actual shooting. He set out to hunt rabbits and loaded his gun for the job.

About then, Maran jumped out from behind one of the ranch buildings and shouted, "Draw!"

Jack's muscle memory took over. He pulled his gun and shot Maran in the shoulder.

Sometimes we think that if it's a game or a joke, our words and actions don't matter. I've had people treat me unkindly and then say, "It was just a joke. Stop being so serious." Have you ever seen that a friend wasn't having fun during a rowdy game and tried to laugh their feelings away? The Bible says that God takes our words and actions seriously. He doesn't want us hurting others, period. Even if we think something is fun or funny, if it causes harm, God says that it is like a madman shooting a deadly weapon. Serious harm can happen and that matters to God, a lot! So, take a lesson from Jack, who was never able to hold a handgun again without shaking. Take a lesson from Maran, who recovered from his gunshot wound and went on to die as a war hero flying missions over Germany during World War II. Remember that God considers each choice we make and word we say as vitally important.

Dear Lord,

Whenever I want to laugh a friend's hurt off as just a joke, please help me to remember that you care about each and every person you made. Help me to keep in mind that you care deeply about how I treat others. Please remind me that even during games and jokes I need to honor you. Give me the strength to be more like you.

Amen.

8

HUNTING TURKEY AND GETTING A BEAR

*"'The LORD who rescued me from the claws of the lion
and the bear will rescue me from this Philistine!'
Saul finally consented. 'All right, go ahead,' he said. 'And
may the LORD be with you!'"*
1 Samuel 17:37

Grandma Autumn's dad, Ben, was a fast gun. Instead of playing sports or video games as a boy, he practiced shooting. He grew up to become a man with crazy gun skills.

When he became a father, he was still an amazing shot. One year, in the spring, they lived in Arizona up against a vast swath of wild land. The wild turkeys were a good size for frying, and so Ben headed out early in the morning to hunt. He never used a shotgun like normal hunters because he didn't like picking buckshot out of his turkey before frying it. Ben was such a good shot that he simply took the heads right off the turkeys with his 300 Savage rifle.

The lighting was still dim as Ben crept through the forest.

Instead of turkeys, Ben saw a large shadow coming silent but fast down the trail. Was it a cow? It didn't make a sound but charged straight for him.

Out of the forest loomed a massive Grizzly Bear. Ben pulled his rifle up and shot from the hip. He didn't have time to sight his gun, but he'd been practicing all his life and his shot went right through the corner of the bear's eye.

The massive creature fell only three gun-lengths away. Ben packed the skin out and later he and a friend hiked out as much meat as they could. One hind leg each was all these grown men could carry.

Now Ben had shot some huge black bears in his time, but next to that grizzly pelt, those big black bear rugs looked like tiny baby bears.

Autumn rendered the bear grease from one of the hind legs to use for cooking and to oil their boots. She got two gallons of bear grease from a single hind leg.

If Ben had not been practicing with a rifle all his life, he would not have been ready when the bear charged. Bears don't normally attack unprovoked, but occasionally, it happens. Even with his skills, it's a miracle he survived that encounter.

You probably won't face a charging Grizzly Bear. However, what you practice is what you become good at. Before David was king, he practiced protecting his father's sheep from lions and bears, and he also learned to trust the Lord. Practice your skills and trust what you can't control to God.

David developed his ability protecting the flock before he set out to fight a giant. He knew that the Lord had been with him during his daily dangers with the sheep and the Lord would be with him as he faced a giant warrior.

Do the hard work that you can and then trust God each day. King David shows us how to both work hard and trust in a powerful God. That way, when the grizzly charges, you will have both skills to use and faith to trust the Lord's plan.

Dear Lord,

Thank you that we can build our skills for the things that we will face in life. But we especially thank you for being there in the things that we can't control. Help me to cling to you when I face danger. Thank you for rescuing me from a life without you and being with me each day.

Amen.

9

THE HIDDEN STILL

"The time is coming when everything that is covered up will be revealed, and all that is secret will be made known to all. Whatever you have said in the dark will be heard in the light, and what you have whispered behind closed doors will be shouted from the housetops for all to hear!"

Luke 12:2-3

Grandma Autumn was a girl during prohibition days, a time 100 years ago when alcohol was illegal in the United States. In those days, one of their neighbors came over for a visit. Her dad and the neighbor had an uneasy relationship, but they still visited one another since neighbors were few and far between and company was hard to come by. In the course of their conversation, the neighbor got to bragging about his secret still where he made moonshine, or illegal alcohol.

"No one will ever find my still. I've hidden it so well, it's impossible to hunt down," he said.

After the neighbor left, Autumn had a question for her father. "What does a still look like?"

Well, her dad Ben described the pipes and collection devices necessary to make a home brew.

"Oh," she said. "I found one of those."

Curious, Ben took Autumn and her brother Wiley out to where she said the hidden still was tucked away. Sure enough, there it was: the impossible-to-find secret still. Autumn, Wiley, and their dad took that illegal still apart piece by piece and buried it in another location.

Now, I'm not suggesting that you copy Ben's behavior, much less that of their neighbor. Her dad wasn't one for following all the rules, but on that occasion, he had a lot of fun making sure that their neighbor couldn't keep on bragging about his unlawful moonshine.

Jesus says that even the things that we take the most care to hide from others will be revealed one day. What is whispered in secret will someday be shouted to everyone.

Make sure that the things you spend your time doing won't shame you or others if they are shouted from the housetops. Have you said something about a friend to someone else that you wouldn't have said to their face? What about the things you joke about? This can be tricky. It takes work to pause before acting or speaking and consider how we would feel if what we're about to do were in the newspaper or captured on video. If the idea of a post on social media about what you're saying makes your stomach feel squidgy, that's a good clue to stop right away and ask God about it! Who we are in secret should be the same as who we are in front of others. We belong to God either way, and our actions should always honor him.

Dear Lord,

It can be easy to act different when people are watching than how I act in secret. It can be tempting to think that no one will find out about hidden things. But all it took to find that hidden still was a little girl riding her horse through the country for fun. Please help me to be yours even when no one is looking and to always be honorable in what I do. Thank you for your love and care.

Amen.

10

BOUNCING BEHIND A HORSE

"Keep on asking, and you will receive what you ask for.
Keep on seeking, and you will find. Keep on knocking,
and the door will be opened to you.
For everyone who asks, receives. Everyone who seeks, finds.
And to everyone who knocks, the door will be opened. You
parents—if your children ask for a loaf of bread, do you
give them a stone instead? Or if they ask for a fish, do you
give them a snake? Of course not!

So if you sinful people know how to give good gifts to your children, how much more will your heavenly Father give good gifts to those who ask him."
Matthew 7:7-11

G randma Autumn was the youngest in her family and always racing to catch up with her brothers and sisters.

One time, her older siblings were tubing behind Nellie, their dad's horse. How do you go tubing behind a horse?

First, they hooked up a rope to Nellie. Then, they tied an inflated inner tube to the far end of the rope. They got Nellie going at a good clip and rode on the inner tube that was bouncing along behind her.

Was this during the winter when heaping snow drifts would pad any crashes? Nope, this was in the heat of the summer, bouncing across bare dirt.

Autumn desperately wanted a ride.

Eventually, her siblings relented and tossed her up on the inner tube for her own adventure. Nellie took off, the tube bounced across the dirt, and Autumn held on for dear life. It was a blast!

Then, she noticed that they were bouncing toward a small hill.

They bounced closer and closer. Autumn gripped the tube tighter and tighter. Nellie was really going fast now. Nellie zipped past the hill without any trouble.

But that inner tube hit that hill and flipped Autumn up, up, up into the air. Free of the tube, Grandma Autumn came down, down, down. She landed splat on top of the small hill . . . which turned out to be a red anthill!

Autumn sat in the dirt, slapping away the biting ants, while Nellie zipped on, the empty tube bounding around behind.

Autumn's anthill adventure reminds me of praying to God for something that I really want. It can be so frustrating when God's answer is "No" or "Not now" all while what I'm talking to him about looks like the best plan. Whether it is a special experience or item that I know would cheer my heart, a good job, or even healing from injury or sickness, it can seem like God gives good gifts to everyone except us.

But just like a crazy ride bouncing behind a horse that ends in an anthill, we don't have the whole picture. If God says "No" it is for a good reason, even if you can't see why.

Trust that God wants to bless you in the way that is the very best for you. Not with fun that ends in ant bites, but with the most wonderful kinds of gifts.

Dear Lord,

Thank you that we can ask you for anything! I pray that my trust in you will grow, and that I can remember you are a father who loves his children and wants to give the best of presents. Please help me to see your love.

Amen.

11

NELLIE AND THE JACKRABBIT HUNT

"He makes the whole body fit together perfectly. As each part does its own special work, it helps the other parts grow, so that the whole body is healthy and growing and full of love."
Ephesians 4:16

Nellie was an incredible horse. Smart, fast, and tame. Nellie even helped Grandma Autumn and her dad hunt jackrabbits.

Grandma's dad, Ben, raised turkeys for a time. Now, you can't feed turkeys only grain. They also need protein or they'll start pecking each other until they are badly injured. To prevent this, Ben needed to feed them a bit of meat now and again. He decided the best way to do this was to hunt some jackrabbits.

Autumn and Nellie both had important jobs when they hunted jackrabbits.

Nellie was used to a hunter shooting directly off her back. She wasn't startled by the gun, and she knew to always keep her head down and away from any flying bullets.

Autumn would ride in the back, hanging onto her dad around the waist. Her first job was to spot the jack rabbits where they were hiding.

When she spotted a rabbit, Autumn would point it out. Ben would turn Nellie toward the rabbit and then the excitement began.

Nellie took her job seriously.

She would explode after that jackrabbit.

Nellie would run full tilt, dodging sagebrush, and zipping left then right then left again as she chased the jackrabbit down. Ben didn't need to direct her with the reins because Nellie knew they were chasing rabbits and did the job all by herself! Autumn would hold on tight until her dad had a clear shot.

Ben shot right off of Nellie's back, from the hip most of the time, and he was such a good shot that he'd get those rabbits right through the eye.

Once he'd shot the rabbit, Autumn would get down, scramble over to grab the rabbit, and then climb back up. They would shoot about twelve jackrabbits at a time. Then Ben, Autumn, and Nellie would head on home.

Did you notice how Ben, Autumn, and Nellie all worked together? Ben was a crazy good shot with a rifle. Autumn picked up many a jackrabbit over the years, all of them shot off a moving horse and through the eye. Autumn was pretty brave herself, hanging onto a charging horse that was cutting left and then right at high speeds. Then there was Nellie. Most horses need some direction from their rider. All that Nellie needed was for Ben to point out a jackrabbit and then off she'd charge! Just like it took three amazing individuals to bring home dinner for the turkeys, it takes many different kinds of people with many different kinds of gifts to work in God's kingdom. Remember that God made you unique and for a purpose!

He has given you special talents that will bring you joy when you use them and bless others!

Dear Lord,

Sometimes I can get jealous. I don't shoot like Ben did or ride a horse like Autumn. Please help me to remember that you have made me with gifts and abilities that no one else has. You have tasks for me to do that are important. Give me the strength to do them and joy in being a part of your kingdom.

Amen.

12

A FANCY DRESS AND A BROKEN LEG

"What sorrow awaits you teachers of religious law and you Pharisees. Hypocrites! For you are like whitewashed tombs—beautiful on the outside but filled on the inside with dead people's bones and all sorts of impurity. Outwardly you look like righteous people, but inwardly your hearts are filled with hypocrisy and lawlessness."

Matthew 23:27-28

When Grandma Autumn was three years old, they had a big flower box outside one of the windows at their house. It was starting to pull away from the building, which made it incredibly fun. Autumn would run up to that planter box, jump, and hang from it, springing up and down.

However, her dad saw her bouncing one day. "Don't do that again. I'm heading to town, but I'll fix it when I get back."

He left for town, but Autumn was still eyeing that flower box. Her dad was about to fix her fun toy. That flower box would never be available for bouncing again. One more bounce wouldn't hurt.

One more bounce absolutely did hurt.

The flower box fell off the wall and landed right on top of Autumn. It broke her leg and smashed her face in the dirt. To make things worse, this flower box was so big she couldn't get free. It took two of her older siblings to lift the heavy planter box off her body.

Autumn's older sister Emma was in charge. As a responsible adult, what do you think she did first? If you guessed "Get Autumn medical care" then you would be wrong. The first thing Emma did . . . get her little sister cleaned up and then carefully dressed in a brand-new gown she'd just sewn for young Autumn that had never been worn.

Never mind the crying and the broken leg, appearances had to be addressed first. What would people say if they saw her little sister wearing an old dress and covered in dirt? After all this important primping had happened, Emma took Autumn to town to get her leg set.

For an active little girl, sitting in bed for weeks waiting to heal was the worst part of the experience. Because of this, Autumn was given the only small dog their family ever owned. A Jack Russel terrier that she named Spot. Spot helped her through having to stay in bed and was a special friend for many years.

What do you think? What was the most important thing for Emma to do when Autumn got hurt? Get Autumn's broken leg looked at by a doctor or get her all fancied up in a new dress?

Jesus talked about how we sometimes care too much about outward appearances when we are trying to follow God. He said that when people just want to look good instead of actually doing good things, it was like they were putting fresh clean paint on tombs, places full of rotting bones that were not clean no matter how much paint was used. It was like washing the outside of a cup and leaving a bunch of guck on the inside, the part that you actually drink from. Jesus told his followers to worry about what really mattered. To actually live good lives instead of just look like they were living good lives. God values an honest heart and true kindness.

Dear Lord,

Please help me to avoid getting sidetracked making myself look all fancy and good. Help me to actually be good in my heart and in the way I treat others. Give me your strength to love people well.

Amen.

13

OLD TIMEY FESTIVITIES

"The Spirit of the LORD is upon me, for he has anointed me to bring Good News to the poor.
He has sent me to proclaim that captives will be released, that the blind will see,
that the oppressed will be set free, and that the time of the LORD's favor has come."
Luke 4:18-19

W hen Grandma Autumn was a girl, the town she lived in loved to celebrate the 4th of July.

To start the day off, there was an old bachelor who liked to wake the whole town at dawn on Independence Day. He would wrangle up a stick of dynamite, because apparently folks just had those lying around back then. He'd grab an old, metal, five-gallon bucket for safety (safety first) and then go out into the middle of the big dirt street that ran through the middle of town.

This fellow would light his stick of dynamite, toss it down in the street, put the bucket over the top, and then stand back.

Boom!

The explosion would wake everyone and let them know that it was the 4th of July! Of course, it would also blow a crater in the street, so part of their celebration was filling in that year's hole with a shovel.

After that, the whole town gathered for a pancake feed. The people working the griddle didn't bother bringing you a pancake. Nope, folks were expected to participate back then.

The flapjack flippers would cook a pancake and then just flip it in the general direction of a hungry person with an empty plate. Folks were in charge of getting their plate underneath the flying flapjack!

Autumn said that the flapjack flippers were actually pretty accurate, and most people managed to snag their pancakes out of the air, although there were always a few mishaps.

When Jesus stood up in the synagogue and read the Bible passage from Isaiah that we see in Luke chapter four, he was letting everyone know that they finally had something to truly celebrate. The Messiah himself had come, and he was in the business of proclaiming freedom! Not the freedom of the U.S. from Great Britain, or the freedom of Israel from the Romans. No, this was the kind of freedom that only our Creator can give. Good news for the poor, freedom for prisoners, recovery of sight for blind eyes, release for the oppressed, and a proclamation that the Lord had noticed them and looked upon them with favor.

Do you ever feel alone, unnoticed, battered and buffeted from every side, unable to see good around you? Do you have trouble trusting that God looks upon you with love? Yeah, that's how the people in Israel were feeling, too. Jesus was letting the people know that their Messiah had come and not just for the wealthy and the powerful, but for those who were pushed aside by society and forgotten.

If you are feeling forgotten today, I want you to remember something worth celebrating, worth waking the whole town with a boom! God sees you. He has come for you. He is the shepherd and the healer and the rescuer. Will you let loose and celebrate? Will you follow him today?

Dear Lord,

It is easy to feel overlooked and forgotten. On dark days, please remind me that you came to set captives free and proclaim the Lord's favor! Give me the strength to follow you and to know that I have something that is truly worth celebrating.

Amen.

14

STALLION TROUBLE

"We destroy every proud obstacle that keeps people from knowing God. We capture their rebellious thoughts and teach them to obey Christ."

2 Corinthians 10:5

When Autumn was a girl, folks rode stallions more often than they do now. A stallion can be an incredibly valuable animal, though they're often temperamental. Autumn's dad had one and so did their neighbor. Her mother's family kept a stallion as well.

Autumn's mother, Georgia, used to tease their stallion by climbing through the rafters in the barn above his stall. Apparently, he was a volatile creature because this stallion kept lunging up and trying to bite Georgia and pull her down. The family believed that if he'd gotten her, much stomping and trampling would occur and so Georgia was not allowed near his stall. However, this rule did not keep young Georgia out of the rafters.

She wore a long skirt that swung down as she climbed, and one time the stallion grabbed it. He yanked. Georgia held on and the stallion pulled her skirt right off. Georgia escaped being trampled, but it wasn't safe to retrieve her skirt as the stallion was busy stomping it. She had to run across the property and sneak into the house, without her skirt. Georgia was caught and it was clear what she'd been doing because her skirt was discovered back in the barn.

Hearing her mother's tales did not make Autumn a more cautious little girl.

When she was about twelve, Autumn decided to go on a ride with the neighbor girl. The neighbor took her to their stable to pick a mount. Well, Autumn immediately knew which horse she wanted to ride. A gorgeous red roan stallion who looked like he had some spunk.

"No one really rides that horse but my father," her friend said. "I'm not sure if we're allowed."

This information did not cause Autumn to want a different horse! So, they saddled him up, and both girls went on a nice long ride.

Well, he was indeed spunky. Autumn had to keep on her toes while riding but she managed just fine and they had a wonderful time.

When the girls got back, there was a whole group of men gathering out front preparing a search party. Why? The stallion was a known man-killer. The thought that a twelve-year-old girl had saddled up this powerful animal sent all the local men into a frenzy. They were terrified for Autumn's life.

Autumn's friend got into huge trouble for letting her ride her father's stallion because he was indeed a lively animal and had killed two men.

However, it turned out that this spirited horse, the man-killer, was nothing a twelve-year-old girl with a firm but gentle way of riding couldn't handle.

Thoughts can be incredibly dangerous and lead us down a path of pain and brokenness, much like a stomping, biting stallion. But Autumn's confident and gentle hand put that dangerous horse through his paces. Instead of raging and fighting, seek the Lord's help in capturing every thought and giving it to him. Victory over our thoughts is ours with God giving us his kind of strength.

Dear Lord,

When my thoughts start raging, leading me down a dark path, and making me feel small and helpless, please remind me that you give us the strength to take every thought captive. That we don't have to shout and fight, that a quiet confidence in you can take control of those thoughts once more. Thank you for your gentleness and your power in our lives.

Amen.

15

THOSE PESKY PRANKS

"Because of God's grace to me, I have laid the foundation like an expert builder. Now others are building on it. But whoever is building on this foundation must be very careful."
I Corinthians 3:10

Grandma Autumn's dad, Ben, was known for playing pranks. Sometimes they backfired, though. Emma, one of Autumn's older sisters, decided to go to a party one evening. She walked to town through an alfalfa field. Her dad knew what time she'd be coming back. So, he grabbed a bear rug and hid in the alfalfa next to the path. With the rug slung over his back and the bear's head positioned on top of his head, Ben looked very much like an actual bear. Emma came walking back from the party, alone, through the dark alfalfa field. Now, Emma was a young woman, about twenty at the time and only five feet tall. However, when Ben rose up out of the alfalfa with that bear rug over his head and gave a menacing growl, she didn't run. Nope, Autumn's sister picked up a rock and just about clunked her dad over the head before he could let her know it was him!

Even though Ben played many tricks on all his kids, none of Autumn's siblings were brave enough to play tricks back on their dad, except Emma.

In the winter, Ben had to cut a hole in the ice that crusted the river so their cattle could drink. One frosty morning, he was concerned that one of his cows had calved in the night. So, he and Emma went out looking for the cow and a possible newborn calf.

They walked along the river and out onto the thick ice, looking for any sign of the new mother.

"Is that a calf's leg, sticking up out of the ice?" Emma asked, pointing.

Ben looked, but couldn't tell. Was it just a stick or a calf's leg?

"Here, look from this angle." Emma suggested he move over a little and then a little more and then back a few steps until . . .

Ben fell right into the hole he had cut in the ice for the cows!

Now this happened in the deep of winter and it was dangerously cold.

Emma dragged her dad out of the water and got him back to their cabin. His clothes were frozen stiff to his body, but once they made it back to the cabin everyone scrambled to get him warmed up.

An incredibly dangerous prank, but one they eventually ended up laughing about for years to come.

The Bible tells us to be careful how we build our lives. We make choices that change who we are and that affect those around us. Children are especially prone to copy the things their parents do and say. Does your speech glorify God? What about your actions? Autumn's dad built a legacy of traps and tricks over his lifetime. When his pesky daughter Emma came along, those tricks came back to bite him! Be very cautious as you build your life, God cares about who we are and who we'll grow to be. Build a life that honors him.

Dear Lord,

Please help me to remember that how I live leaves a legacy. That my actions affect those around me and even those who will come after me. Give me wisdom to choose words and deeds that will build a life that glorifies you and your kingdom.

Amen.

16

WILL YOU SHOOT AGAINST MY GIRLS?

"'Don't worry about this Philistine,' David told Saul. 'I'll go fight him!'

'Don't be ridiculous!' Saul replied. 'There's no way you can fight this Philistine and possibly win! You're only a boy, and he's been a man of war since his youth.'...

David replied to the Philistine, 'You come to me with sword, spear, and javelin, but I come to you in the name of the LORD of Heaven's Armies—the God of the armies of Israel, whom you have defied.'"

I Samuel 17:32-33 and 45

G randma Autumn had three older sisters and they were all great shots with a rifle. Now, their dad, Ben, was the one who was known for his marksmanship and not many knew that he had passed on his skill to his daughters.

During the fall in the Okanogan Valley in Washington, locals enjoyed competing in turkey shoots.

This was not an event where turkeys were shot, no, this was a marksmanship competition in which the winners got to take home a live turkey just before Thanksgiving . . . which was very convenient for the upcoming Thanksgiving feast.

Everyone wanted to win their turkey rather than purchase one since money was tight during the Great Depression.

Now, all the neighbors were sick and tired of having Ben win a turkey every single year. He was just too good with a gun and it took all of the fun out of the competition.

That year, when he showed up at the turkey shoot with two of his teenage daughters in tow, they told him that he was disqualified. No one was willing to shoot against him.

"Sure, sure. But . . . are you willing to shoot against my girls?"

Well, this group of men couldn't quite bring themselves to disqualify two teenage girls from competing against all those guys. What would it look like if they refused?

So, Autumn's older sisters got to compete in the turkey shoot.

That year, instead of her dad bringing home a turkey, like always, both of her sisters brought home a turkey each. The girls enjoyed the fun of competitive shooting and their family enjoyed two free turkeys instead of one.

Now, just like that group of men underestimated Autumn's sisters, King Saul underestimated the shepherd boy, David. Even more concerning though, Saul underestimated God. Saul should have known that God could use even the scrawniest of shepherd boys to beat the mightiest warrior in the land. In fact, why hadn't Saul hopped into his own armor and marched out there against Goliath, knowing and trusting that God was capable against this merely human foe?

So many times, we trust what our eyes can see over what God has told us in his word about who he is, what he can do, and how he feels about his children. Don't be the one who underestimates all that God can do. Just like a shepherd boy who beats a giant, just like a pair of teenage girls who outshoot all the men, God surprises us again and again.

Dear Lord,

It is easy to be overwhelmed by what I can see around me and forget what I cannot fathom. You stand with mighty angel armies and even so, you love your children deeply and will fight on their behalf. Please help me not to underestimate you and all that you want to do in my life and in the lives of those around me. Give me the strength to believe.

Amen.

17

FANCY DOODADS

"So he returned home to his father. And while he was still a long way off, his father saw him coming. Filled with love and compassion, he ran to his son, embraced him, and kissed him."

Luke 15:20

M en from older generations seemed to only val-ue useful items. Perhaps it came from being in charge of families during the Great Depression, but what-ever the reason, it was frustrating for the women in their lives once times got better and there was spending money available.

One of Grandma's relatives would only plant things you could eat. His wife loved flowers . . . but he planted a huge garden full of vegetables.

Grandpa Del's dad, George, wouldn't buy his wife anything silver. Rosa loved silver and eventually ended up buying herself her own set of silverware when she was in her fifties.

Because her in-laws didn't own anything silver, Grandma Autumn thought that her mother-in-law must consider it a waste of money. Autumn had purchased two silver spoons, one for herself and one for Del that they used for special occasions. Rosa came to help when Autumn was in the hospital having a baby. Autumn hid the spoons from her mother-in-law so she wouldn't have to face her disapproval.

Well, as part of her plan to help, Rosa completely reorganized all the kitchen cupboards. "You'll like it better like this," she said.

She discovered Autumn's silver spoons hidden in an out-of-the-way cupboard. But Rosa wasn't upset about the three-dollar spoons. She was thrilled that her daughter-in-law appreciated beautiful things and immediately went out and bought her some more silver spoons!

Autumn couldn't find anything in her cupboards . . . but she had more pretty spoons.

I think that sometimes we are like this with God. We expect a stern response from him, scowling eyebrows, roaring thunder, maybe a smiting lightning bolt, or at the very least a circle of angels shaking their heads at our failures.

Remember though, this is the God that Jesus himself described as a father. A father who spotted his wayward son from a long way off and ran down the road to snatch that boy into his arms and give him a rib-cracking hug. This is a father who threw a party when his broken and bedraggled son came home. Jesus says this is what God is like. According to Jesus, even the angels join in the party when someone chooses to come to God.

Do you think the worst of God?

What if he loves you more than you can even imagine? Are you going to trust what you think God might be like or what Jesus himself said about his father?

Dear Lord,

Sometimes I think you must be disgusted with my mistakes and with me, as well. Help me to remember what Jesus said you are like when my mistakes seem so big and you seem so far away. Help me to remember the story about a father who runs and hugs his lost son and throws a party. Thank you for your love and for rushing out to meet the runaway.

Amen.

18

Pudgy the Hunting Dog

"Yes, the body has many different parts, not just one part. If the foot says, 'I am not a part of the body because I am not a hand,' that does not make it any less a part of the body. And if the ear says, 'I am not part of the body because I am not an eye,' would that make it any less a part of the body? If the whole body were an eye, how would you hear? Or if your whole body were an ear, how would you smell anything? But our bodies have many parts, and God has put each part just where he wants it."

I Corinthians 12:14-18

My grandparents both loved dogs. However, Delbert wanted a useful dog and Autumn wanted a snuggly dog.

One day, Del was looking through the newspaper and saw that someone had dropped a fine hunting dog off at the local pound. Now that was a useful dog!

So, he asked Autumn to go on down to the pound to check out that hunting dog while Del was at work.

Autumn journeyed to the pound on her mission of mercy.

However, back in those days, the pound had a drop box out front so people could leave their unwanted pets when the pound was closed. The workers would just check the box every morning to see if any new animals had arrived.

Well, Autumn walked towards the front door and noticed that someone had dropped a dog in the box overnight.

Shivering and wet, a small dog with a fat body and teeny tiny legs sat alone in the wire box. She had been there all night, alone, after the only people she knew had decided they didn't want her anymore.

Autumn's chest grew tight. This was not the dog that Del wanted. She had been sent on a very specific mission to acquire a useful dog. However, she could not leave that poor little animal alone in the cold.

And so, Autumn came home with Pudgy. An animal who was most definitely not a hunting dog.

However, Pudgy was a loving and loyal companion to the family for the rest of her days. She might not have been the dog they wanted, but she was the dog who wanted them and needed them. Rescuing Pudgy from the drop box brought their whole family incredible joy.

Not everyone has the same gifts, the Bible says that if God made you a foot you shouldn't be complaining that you are not a hand.

Pudgy wasn't a hunting dog, but God made her wonderful all the same. She was a loving and loyal friend.

Dear Lord,

Thank you for making me on purpose. Thank you for having a plan for how I can honor you, no matter how hard the days get. Give me the strength to please you all my days, just like Pudgy loved her people so very well.

Amen.

PART 2

DEL'S STORIES

Delbert Elmer Griffith was my paternal grandfather and the son of George Griffith (a quiet baseball fan who liked to shoot flies off the wall) and Rosa White (a tough negotiator who always got a good deal for their livestock). Del married Autumn in 1942 and they had four children, including my dad who was their youngest. Del was the hardest worker I have ever met. Even up into his 80's, he could work the young men who came to help into the ground. Del came to know God in his 50s and left life as a milkman to start Camas Meadows Bible Camp with Autumn and her sister Lily. My husband and I now live in their log home (he felled trees from their own land and skinned the logs for this house by hand) and work at the camp they started. So grab your ax and get some wood split while Del tells you a tale.

19

THE ROWDY SUITOR

"Don't copy the behavior and customs of this world, but let God transform you into a new person by changing the way you think. Then you will learn to know God's will for you, which is good and pleasing and perfect . . . Don't let evil conquer you, but conquer evil by doing good."

Romans 12:2, 21

G randpa Del loved to tell the story of how his father courted his mother, way back in 1910.

There are many reasons a father might get frustrated with a young man who has come to romance his daughter. Maybe he thinks the young man's hair is strange, doesn't think he makes enough money, or dislikes his taste in music. However, the reasons that Rosa's father was frustrated with his daughter's suitor were from a completely different era.

George made two mistakes.

First, when he came courting, he didn't eat what was set before him with a grateful heart. Nope, he asked for sugar on his beans.

Second, George wasted a whole bunch of ammunition by doing a fair bit of target practice . . . in the house! He kept shooting flies off the walls with his pistol. Was George trying to prove to his future father-in-law that he would be a good protector? Was he hoping to impress Rosa with his fancy shooting? No one knows.

How did Rosa's father react?

The man shook his head with frustration when George showed off, shooting flies off the walls. But when he dared to ask for sugar on his beans, Rosa's dad told George that if he wanted sugar for his beans, he could bring his own sugar! Shooting a fly or two was one thing, but asking for sugar . . . now that was insulting.

Well, George did bring his own sugar and was allowed to continue seeing Rosa.

Now, I wouldn't have had any problem grabbing some sugar for George's beans. However, I would not have taken kindly to him shooting flies off my walls! My definition of bad behavior is completely different from Rosa's dad's. Thankfully, we don't have to rely on each other's idea of what bad behavior is. God has provided a guide in his Bible, telling us all about right and wrong.

Grandpa Del thought that Rosa's little family cabin in Idaho must have been full of holes after all that fly shooting, but regardless, his parents married in 1911 and raised a big family of their own. Grandpa Del was never allowed to do his target practice in the house, though.

Dear Lord,

Sometimes it is hard to tell what is right from what is wrong. It feels wrong when something really upsets me, like a visitor who doesn't like the taste of the pot of beans I just made. Give me your wisdom to see if I might be ignoring a dangerous situation because something else bothered me more. Please remind me to read in your Bible about right and wrong so that I can look at the situation with wisdom. Thank you for leading me toward your truth and for helping me to follow you.

Amen.

20

THE BIG MOVE

"The Lord had said to Abram, 'Leave your native country, your relatives, and your father's family, and go to the land that I will show you. I will make you into a great nation. I will bless you and make you famous, and you will be a blessing to others.'"
Genesis 12:1-2

During the Great Depression, the land Grandpa Del's family lived on started to dry up.

Since they couldn't look at new property online, Del's dad George took off on his horse to investigate a spot up in Canada. They didn't have a doctor or a school, so George kept looking. He finally found a place just over the Canadian border and the entire family prepared to leave.

They had a Studebaker car and a horse-drawn wagon with iron wheels that they'd purchased from Sears. George wanted a spare wheel, so he ordered one from the Sears catalog. It didn't arrive, so he ordered another. The same thing happened again. He kept ordering until the wagon wheel finally showed up . . . along with four more!

Del's mother Rosa sold their extra livestock since George was a quiet man who didn't always get the best price. Rosa wouldn't give up or give in and always walked away from the stock dealers with a good deal.

While making these preparations, they bought a horse that wasn't broken to the harness. Though it was hitched with a more experienced animal, both horses bolted, ran into a post, and caused injury and mayhem. Despite the havoc this caused, the family was soon on their way.

Del didn't sit in the car or the covered wagon as they traveled from Tonasket up into Canada. He rode his mare with her colt, Snip, tagging along behind. They saw their first paved road in the town of Agassiz, British Columbia. New sights in a new land. However, their horses did not approve. The animals didn't like walking on the paved roads one bit!

Hearing Grandpa Del tell about their Depression-Era journey helps me imagine Abraham traveling to a new land. It wouldn't have been easy to obey. While Abraham and Sarah didn't have six children, they took their nephew Lot and shepherds to watch their flocks. Moving that amount of stock is tough, as Grandpa's story about the stampeding horses explains. Was Abraham as crafty a dealmaker as Rosa or did he sent someone else to haggle out the price for their extra livestock? Regardless of the upheaval, Abraham listened to God's call and obeyed.

Would you?

God might not ask you to travel to a new land, but he absolutely does have important tasks for each of his children. God asked me to follow my parents to the mountains when he called them to start a summer camp ministry. What if God asks you to forgive a friend who never bothered to say they were sorry? What if he wants you to give up getting a new video game so you can help someone who's hungry? What if he asks you to help a student who struggles with math instead of watching TV? It is never easy. But the hard path is the best path when it's where God wants you. Will you leave behind what is safe and journey toward what God has asked you to do?

Dear Lord,

Please give me the ears to recognize your call and the strength to obey. When you ask me to love and listen and walk a new path, give me a tender heart toward you and the people you put in my life.

Amen.

21

THE MAN WHO LIVED IN A STUMP

"Store your treasures in heaven, where moths and rust cannot destroy, and thieves do not break in and steal. Wherever your treasure is, there the desires of your heart will also be."
Matthew 6:20-21

When my grandpa Del was a boy, he knew a man named Norman Earl who lived in a tree stump. The stump was massive, hollow, and had a roof built over the top. Norman Earl didn't use it as a temporary cabin or a fort. It was his permanent home. He lived there with his cat and an incredibly fine set of china that had come from Russia during the time of the Czars.

Norman's family lived in England after fleeing Russia and had a large home with "cooks and maids and all" as my grandpa told it. Norman was highly educated in England, before moving to the United States. Grandpa Del said they left Russia "when the Czar had taken over" and I have no idea what he meant by this. Which Czar? Could he be talking about the fall of the Romanov Dynasty in 1917 when Bolshevik revolutionaries killed the royal family? Or perhaps it was earlier, when Czar Nicholas first took the throne. It is hard to say.

Though Norman lived in the forest alone with his cat, he enjoyed having visitors to his tree stump and loved to pull pranks on any unsuspecting person willing to stop by.

He had been injured as a child and his right hand jumped and wobbled so that he couldn't hold it still. He delighted in offering to shake hands and then watching his visitor try to dive and capture hold of his bobbing arm so they could shake back.

Norman was injured as a child, a refugee from the nation he loved, living in a makeshift home so tight he had to open a special window for his feet to stick out from the end of his bed, with only the family china left from his former life of opulence, but he found laughter in the very difficulties that plagued him.

Del loved to visit Norman, hearing stories from a time long passed and drinking tea from that fancy china in Norman's tree stump.

Wealth is fleeting. A person can be in a place of power one moment and in poverty the next. Jesus' words in Matthew 6:20-21 are so vital for us to remember when the world is unstable. Wealth is a dangerous thing to set your heart on because you could be pampered and surrounded by servants one day and living in a tree stump the next. However, no matter where he lived or what he owned, Norman was someone who blessed others with his lively conversation and wacky sense of humor. If we are willing to trust him, God will give us strength to live and love others and find joy even in hard times. Seek what is real and important, my friends, just like the man in the stump.

Dear Lord,

Help me to remember that riches and power can disappear in an instant, but a heart that loves and serves you is full of the kind of treasure that lasts forever.

Amen.

22

PLAYING COYOTE AND HUNTER

*"Do not waste time arguing over godless ideas and old wives'
tales. Instead, train yourself to be godly. Physical training
is good, but training for godliness is much better, promising
benefits in this life and in the life to come."*
I Timothy 4:7-8

When my grandfather Delbert and his brothers
were young, he and Stanley decided to play coyote
and hunter. The rules to the game were simple, although
not without peril for those involved. One brother was to

play the hunter. To do so, the boys brought along their slingshots and rocks. The other brother was supposed to play the coyote. This involved prancing around in the sagebrush and howling. The boys planned to switch who got to play the hunter and who was the coyote.

Well, Grandpa Del was the coyote first. So, he sat there behind his sage bush and lifted his nose in a long and mournful howl.

Now, I played many an imaginary game as a child. Clearly, Del was not actually a coyote. One would think that pretending to be the hunter would also require the use of imagination. Apparently, Stanley had a harder time with imaginary games. He set off through the sagebrush with his slingshot and a nice, solid rock. He aimed at the "coyote" and let that rock fly.

The rock hit Grandpa Del right in the mouth, chipping a tooth.

The coyote was howling but not the kind of howling one expects. This was not the mournful song of a wild canine howling at the moon. No, howls of pain filled the land. Then, in a fit of rage, the coyote jumped up, ran through the sagebrush, and tackled the hunter!

Whenever Grandpa Del told that story, he would get a twinkle in his eye and say: "Well, the coyote chased the hunter that day!"

Have you ever acted in a way that you shouldn't have? Acted like the kind of person that you didn't really want to be? Del and his brother were just playing, but in their game they acted out an attack with a slingshot. You shouldn't practice something you don't really want to become.

Delbert's brother practiced zipping that rock right at Del . . . and then he really did it! It is important to practice the things that we truly want to be. The things that will make both God and ourselves proud of who we grow to become in the end.

Dear Lord,

Please show me when I'm practicing something that will not honor you. Help me to practice at being the kind of person I want to become. Give me the strength to grow and be more like you.

Amen.

23

COLD WINTER NIGHTS

*"Fire goes out without wood, and quarrels disappear
when gossip stops.
A quarrelsome person starts fights as easily as hot embers
light charcoal or fire lights wood."*
Proverbs 26:20-21

When Grandpa Del was a boy, his dad George would stoke the stove up real hot on cold winter nights to keep their family warm. The problem? Sometimes the wood had too much pitch in it and would burn so fiercely that the entire stove and its pipe would glow red.

But the real danger didn't happen until that stove started shuddering and moving on its own due to the heat. At that point, the wall behind it might catch fire. In fact, one time, it did!

But George was prepared. He would grab a bucket of water that he kept handy next to the stove. When it started to smoke, George would splash that wall down so it wouldn't catch fire.

Del's mother, Rosa, also prepared for those cold winter nights. She would read to the family from a serial story that ran in the Saturday Evening Post. If it was cold enough, they would go outside to pull vinegar taffy. For this, the children buttered their hands while they waited for the hot candy to cool slightly. Each child then took a lump of taffy outside into the frigid air to pull and pull until the candy turned white and grew too stiff to stretch.

Just like George and Rosa prepared for the cold weather by stoking up the fire super-hot or keeping a nice stock of reading material and candy ingredients to entertain their six children, we can choose what we work to gather fuel for.

A pile of books and a well-packed stove fuels warmth and family closeness. We can either work toward feeding the arguments and quarrels around us or work toward calming angry disputes.

The Bible says that like a fire, quarrels must be fed. Similar to George packing that wood stove so full of dry pitchy wood that it glowed red and sometimes set the wall on fire, gossiping can feed an argument until it is just as hot.

Rosa held onto those special magazine stories and gathered the necessary ingredients for vinegar taffy. She collected good things to help her family during the deep cold of winter. Choose carefully what you stockpile for later. Holding onto a grudge or anger in your heart for another person can build up a bitterness that is colder than the most bitter winter night. Make sure that you are stoking and stocking up on the things that will honor God instead. Just like George and Rosa warmed their family with a crackling stove, reading time, and making candy together, you can gather good things for the people around you instead of anger and bitterness.

Dear Lord,

When I hear interesting tidbits about someone else or want to hang onto the hurt and anger I feel, please remind me about George and Rosa preparing for the deep cold of winter. Help me to only feed the warm fires of kindness, not the scorching heat of gossip and fighting. Help me to store up encouraging words for others instead of keeping anger and hurt in my heart. Help me to be the one to help quarrels die and forgiveness to happen.

Amen.

24

GRANDPA DEL GETS AUTUMN FLOWERS

"Oh, that you had listened to my commands!
Then you would have had peace flowing like a gentle river
and righteousness rolling over you like waves in the sea."
Isaiah 48:18

Grandma Autumn was just finishing up high school when she started dating my grandfather, Delbert. World War II was in full swing and money was tight.

Autumn had a Home Economics assignment and was supposed to make a flower arrangement for the teacher to grade. The problem: she didn't have any flowers.

Del told her that he would find her some flowers for her project, and he did. After his bold promise to save the day, he did indeed show up with a lovely bouquet of incredible blooms.

Autumn got busy arranging them and then brought the bouquet to school for her grade.

However, the teacher looked at her bouquet for a long time before commenting on the beauty of the blossoms. There was a strange and suspicious light of interest in her eyes.

Autumn's nerves were thrumming. What was wrong with her flowers? What had her teacher seen that Autumn had missed? She questioned Del about where exactly he'd gotten them.

Finally, Del confessed. He had walked all around Wenatchee peering over fences into people's yards. After some time, he came across a home with a beautiful flower garden. Then my grandfather jumped the fence, cut the flowers, and hustled those pilfered blooms to my grandmother.

That was bad enough. But even worse, Del had managed to steal flowers out of Autumn's home economics teacher's own yard!

Grandpa Del wasn't feeling very peaceful when he had to confess his thieving ways to Grandma Autumn. Poor Autumn wasn't feeling any of God's peace when she faced her home economics teacher the next day! Not only would Del's righteousness have improved if he'd paid attention to God's commands, especially the eighth commandment that has a thing or two to say about stealing, but God promises in the Bible that a special peace comes for those who do the right thing.

Sure, we may see a whole lot of trouble and live through stressful situations. Del and Autumn were courting during World War II, which certainly included trying times. But if he hadn't hopped a fence and stolen some flowers, Del would have had peace about where he'd gotten blooms for the girl he was trying to impress. As it was, he caused her a whole lot of trouble when his ironic theft came to light!

God is not in the business of just thinking up rules so we have to stay on our toes. He offers guidance in his word so that our lives and the lives of those around us are better. He wants good things for his children. Peace and righteousness and joy. If you see a command in the Bible that seems like it's there just to ruin your fun, take a moment to consider the heart of God and how much he loves each one of his children. Your day just might be a bit more peaceful if you do. Grandpa Del's sure would have been!

Dear Lord,

There are days when your commands seem like a lot of trouble and obeying them feels like a whole lot of work. Please remind me of your love and how much you want good things for your children. Please give me a mind and heart that is careful to consider your commands as I choose what to do each day.

Amen.

PART 3

STORIES FROM A MOUNTAIN MEADOW

Many of my grandparents' most memorable stories are from the camas meadows area or what they referred to as either "up on the meadow" or "up on the mountain." You see, Camas Meadows Bible Camp is situated on a mountain meadow. At 3,000 feet above sea level, there is a glorious stretch of meadow right in the foothills of the Cascade Mountains. Rolling meadow grass studded with wildflowers and the occasional island of aspen trees are surrounded by dark hills covered with a pine and fir forest. Autumn's sister Lily and her husband Clarence bought an old dairy farm and the meadow graced the center of their property. Del and Autumn often visited and enjoyed many adventures there with them. Eventually, Lily gave her sister Autumn a unique birthday present. Eighty acres of meadow and forest land. When Del came to know the Lord in his 50s, he and Autumn gifted the land needed to start Camas Medows Bible Camp. This is the camp where my father lived and died and my husband and I work now. The following are stories that happened "up on the meadow" as Del and Autumn lived a life of horseback rides, bear encounters, and surviving the bitter cold. Up on the meadow they grew into the people who would one day found a Bible camp with 20 acres of undeveloped land

and a whole heap of grit and determination. So grab your mittens, a crosscut saw, and call your favorite horse with a whistle. It's time for tales from a mountain meadow!

25

FORTY-TWO BELOW ZERO WITH A HANDSAW

"Preach the word of God. Be prepared, whether the time is favorable or not. Patiently correct, rebuke, and encourage your people with good teaching."

2 Timothy 4:2

In the winter of 1948 or '49 Del, Autumn, and their four young children (my dad was just a baby) stayed in an old homesteader's cabin up on Camas Meadows with Autumn's sister Lily and her husband Clarence.

They plowed the road using a wooden wedge pulled behind horses, but eventually the snow got too deep and they were snowed in.

They had five feet of snow on the ground when the temperature began to drop until it was forty-two degrees below zero. Now Clarence wasn't one for getting firewood ahead of when he needed it.

Every day, Del and Clarence would take a team of horses and go fell a dead tree, haul it to the cabin, and then spend the rest of the day turning it into firewood with a crosscut saw and a splitting maul.

They kept both fireplaces (one on each end of the cabin) blazing all day and night.

It got so cold that the chinking between the logs would crack like a gunshot and shoot out. They tore apart an old mattress to stuff between the logs to keep the wind and the snow from seeping in.

The heat from the blazing fireplaces would go right up to the roof and melt the snow which would then drain down the logs and immediately freeze again. They had a constant wall of ice on one side of the cabin. The family normally put potatoes by the fire to roast through the night. But even with both fires burning high and hot, instead of warm tasty spuds, by morning their potatoes were frozen.

When it was dark, the adults would play card games by the light of kerosine lamps. Del would play games with the children, hide and seek, horse and cowboy, and cattle rustlers. Grandpa Del was usually the horse.

In March, Delbert snowshoed out and talked with the county about plowing the road, since it wouldn't melt until May. He came back with a county bulldozer and their small family was able to see civilization for the first time in months.

If one of them had broken a bone and been unable to work all day long, every day, the small family would most likely have frozen to death. Not frightened by this experience, my grandparents built their own house on Camas Meadows near where Lily and Clarence had settled. They eventually started a Bible camp there, where my husband and I work.

Well, it took the stern rebuke of some incredibly dangerous weather, but Grandpa Del became a firewood stockpiler! Del would stay two years ahead with his firewood and worked innumerable hours bringing in wood all autumn long.

In the same way, but without nearly freezing to death, I hope that you will come to understand how vital it is to be ready to share God's word. Does someone think that there is no hope? Is there a person in your life who isn't being shown patience? Is someone being unkind? What if that child sitting alone at the lunch table feels forgotten? The Bible is full of stories about how much God longs to gather each one of us into his arms and set us on a path of joy and victory instead of sorrow and defeat.

Dear Lord,

Sometimes the idea of sharing about you feels impossible. Please remind me of your ways. Help me to see your wisdom, power, grace, and love. Give me the strength to share about who you are with those who need you today.

Amen.

26

A Pack Rat Finds a Way

"My old self has been crucified with Christ. It is no longer I who live, but Christ lives in me. So I live in this earthly body by trusting in the Son of God, who loved me and gave himself for me."

Galatians 2:20

M y great aunt Lily was the first to settle at Camas Meadows where our family now lives and works. She bought almost the entire meadow and then purchased a house in a box (all the pieces come on a truck and you just put it together) and built an amazing barn constructed with rock walls along the bottom for the cows and timber siding up top for the hay and tack.

Now, in her amazing barn lived a pack rat.

Aunt Lily was done with that pack rat. It was hauling off all her shiny things and stowing them in a nest somewhere. Pack rats love tools and coins, nails and washers and bolts. They can even pick up and carry off whole wrenches, screwdrivers, and sockets.

Lily was a fierce woman who was not above killing a rodent, no matter how adorable, and so she set out a giant snap trap to do that critter in.

Pack rats are smart. Did you know that? Far smarter than people give them credit for. That rat was not fooled by the snap trap, but it did figure out how to trip it and then steal the bait.

The pack rat gathered a bunch of nuts and bolts and then tossed them at the trap until one of them hit just the right spot and the trap sprung. Then the rat ate the bait.

But he wasn't done yet. That pack rat proceeded to carry the empty trap and the nuts and bolts over to Aunt Lily's house, up her steps, onto her porch, and to her front door.

He then placed the trap, nuts, and bolts onto her doorstep for Lily to find in the morning.

When Christ died to rescue us and make a way for us to belong to God, it changed everything. We could go on with how things have always been (rats snapped in traps) trying the old way to be good enough for God or trust Jesus as he offers something baffling and new. That rat left the old ways behind in a bold way. Jesus is calling us to leave the old ways behind as well, since he died our death and asks us to be free in him, following his ways into life!

Dear Lord,

Thank you for giving me the chance to leave the old person I was behind and become new in you. Please help me to live as a new creature who trusts in your sacrifice and knows that I don't have to live life like I did before, because you have changed everything.

Amen.

27

SUNDANCE AND THE CHICKENS

"What sorrow awaits you teachers of religious law and you Pharisees. Hypocrites! For you shut the door of the Kingdom of Heaven in people's faces. You won't go in yourselves, and you don't let others enter either."

Matthew 23:13

My horse Sundance was pesky and he was smart. Sundance was pesky and smart long before I owned him, back when he was Grandpa Del's horse. But that didn't mean he couldn't be tricked.

When Del and Autumn first bought him, he was a spirited gray gelding who was half Arabian and half quarter horse. He pranced when he trotted and held his tail high. He had a high-pitched whistling snort and he loved to dance sideways about imagined dangers.

Sundance had also never encountered farm life or barnyard animals. He had a lot to learn.

When they first put him in the corral with the other horses, Sundance figured he could steal everyone else's grain. He ran and he nipped and he chased until every other horse was herded over to the far side of the corral.

Then Sundance pranced back to the feed trough to enjoy the spoils of his piracy.

Only, the chickens had flapped up into the trough and they were eating all the grain. Never having encountered chickens before, Sundance wasn't sure if they were dangerous predators or not? They certainly seemed confident.

Too frightened to risk the chickens' wrath, Sundance watched from a distance as they ate all of his "rightfully stolen" grain. And that is how the chickens made a chicken of a thousand-pound horse.

This tale of horsey antics reminds me of something far more serious. In Matthew, Jesus talks about some folks who were chasing people away from following him. But they weren't doing all of this chasing because they wanted the first shot at following Jesus. Nope, they refused to accept Jesus as their Lord and even worse, they didn't want anyone else to either. Just like Sundance never got his extra oats, these religious leaders and Pharisees refused the joy of following their Messiah and spent their time chasing others away. These were people who believed in God! People who had studied and taught God's word all their lives. They were considered experts on all things about God, but they didn't recognize him when he called them to follow.

You are unlikely to see people running up to folks and shouting, "Get away from Jesus!" But even without doing that, church folks can still chase others away from our Lord.

Have you ever let anger make you forget that you belong to Jesus? What about when someone is unkind or rude? What if someone else doesn't agree with you about something important, does that make it feel OK to treat them badly? Yep, this can chase folks away from Jesus just like Sundance chasing the other horses and those silly chickens keeping him from the oats.

Dear Lord,

This is such a hard thing to think about. People who follow you, actually chasing folks away from your love. Me, chasing folks away from belonging to you! Please give me sharp eyes to see right away if I begin to do this. Help the fruits of your Spirit change the way I behave. Fill me with your love, joy, peace, patience, kindness, goodness, faithfulness, gentleness, and self-control so that others are drawn to you and not pushed away. Give me the strength for this as I know I'm not able on my own.

Amen.

28

PRIDE GOETH BEFORE THE CRASH

"Pride goes before destruction, and haughtiness before a fall."
Proverbs 16:18
"As for the rest of you, dear brothers and sisters, never get tired of doing good."
2 Thessalonians 3:13

S undance was the most curious horse my grandparents owned. Once, a friend of theirs asked if he could hunt on their property. They told him, yes, but that he shouldn't park his pickup truck so close to the horse corral.

"We have a very curious horse and he gets into things," they explained.

"I know all about curious horses," their friend said. "There isn't anything in there that he can hurt." He then headed out to go hunting, confident in his knowledge about horses and their curiosity level.

Sundance immediately trotted over to investigate his truck.

After a short time, Grandma Autumn and Grandpa Del heard a crash from out by the corral.

Sundance had found the man's toolbox, picked it up by the handle in his teeth, and then dropped it into the snow.

Tools went everywhere!

When their friend got back, they saw him grumbling to himself while he picked up tools out of the snow drifts. He didn't get them all though, because they found a bunch more in the spring!

There are so many things we can learn from the stories around us, but I'll just point out two here. Del and Autumn attempted to give their friend a warning based on their special knowledge about Sundance. But he was so confident in his own experience with horses that he was too proud to listen. He couldn't imagine that they might know something that he did not.

Now, my horse Sundance never tired of being pesky and causing trouble. He didn't become mine until he was twenty-two years old, but he was still a trickster. My friends, never tire of doing what is right! If Sundance could live to the ripe old age of thirty-two and keep on pulling pranks all that time, you too can persevere. You can follow Jesus with the same determination that Sundance showed as he caused so much trouble for many, many years!

Dear Lord,

Please keep my heart from pride and help me to listen to others and search out if they have some wisdom to share. Let me be as determined to do good as Sundance was determined to cause trouble. Thank you for the wonderful stories all around us and how they can lead me to you!

Amen

29

BLUFF CHARGED

"Fear of the LORD is the foundation of true wisdom.
All who obey his commandments will grow in wisdom.
Praise him forever!"
Psalm 111:10

G randma Autumn used to tell the story of how she was bluff charged by a bear. It usually came up because a child, new to the forest, asked what to do if they saw a bear in the woods. Autumn would listen quietly to the child's fears and then reply. "With a cougar, be brave. With a bear, be humble." Because she knew from experience that while shouting and waving your arms will most likely spook a big cat, this approach doesn't always work for a bear. There are moments when respect is the best choice.

Autumn was out on a walk, enjoying the old logging roads and game trails that crisscross the forests that surround our mountain meadow. As she came around a corner, Autumn spotted something near the path. An elk's head, just lying there, half eaten. How interesting. She crept closer. What had killed the elk? As Autumn investigated, a black bear appeared.

The bear burst from the cover of the forest and barreled straight for her, running at full speed. Now, a bear has a lot of weight behind him, and they can go fast! But right before he hit her, the bear skidded to a stop. He was only a few feet away.

The bear let out a deep huff and pounded the ground with his front feet.

The worst response would have been to scream and run away. And in this instance, shouting and making herself look bigger like she would for a cougar, was no way to answer the bear's clear communication.

Instead, Autumn showed respect for the bear by backing up slowly with her eyes lowered until she could step behind a tree. She knew this was a bluff charge. The polite—but stern—way that bears tell folks to move along.

The bear lumbered back to his elk, pleased that Grandma Autumn understood.

The lessons of the forest often make me think about the lessons found in the Bible.

Do you fear God? Not a fear that makes you run away screaming, but a fear that leads you to listen and show him respect. Now, God isn't a bear, thank goodness! But think about how Autumn showed respect for the bear on her forest walk. Thankfully, through Jesus, God has made a way for us to look him straight in the eye, despite how awesome and powerful he is. God isn't a bear guarding his dinner. But God wants our respect as well as our love. Remember Grandma Autumn's wise response to the powerful bear and listen to a mighty God when he tells you the right path to take.

Dear Lord,

Help me to remember how mighty and powerful you are. Please give me the strength to let go of my pride and listen to your words. Guide me in your ways and help me to obey your wisdom.

Amen.

30

THE HORSE WHO LOVED SLEDDING

"For I am about to do something new. See, I have already
begun! Do you not see it?
I will make a pathway through the wilderness. I will create
rivers in the dry wasteland. The wild animals in the fields
will thank me, the jackals and owls, too, for giving them
water in the desert.
Yes, I will make rivers in the dry wasteland so my chosen
people can be refreshed."
Isaiah 43:19-20

Grandpa Del was out in the forest one day, staying at a remote cabin with some friends. Since it was a hunting trip, they'd brought their horses along. If anyone shot a deer, the horses would help haul the meat home before it spoiled.

Among these horses was one of their favorites, Skookum. She was a funny little mare who loved to eat sugar cookies and had even snorked down an entire box of peaches, carefully spitting out every pit before diving into the box for more juicy fruit. She had the odd quirk of falling over for no reason, even with a rider on her back. Autumn simply warned new riders that they should be ready to jump clear if Skookum started to topple.

It was a secluded area and Del expected to see wild animals and wild animal tracks. What they did not expect, a single strange track that dug a shallow trench down the hillside near their campsite. The track resembled a long slide mark down the hill from top to bottom. Had a cougar dragged a dead animal past them in the night?

Later, Skookum wandered away from the rest of the horses. Del saw movement from the forest. Here came

Skookum, head first and upside down, sliding down the hill with her hooves straight up in the air!

Poor girl, had she fallen?

At the bottom of the hill Skookum stood up, shook herself off, trudged back to the top, and then slid down again! She did this several times, just for the pure fun of it!

Are you sometimes confused by things that happen? What is God up to? Why did he let something hard occur? Why didn't he fix a person or a situation that was broken? Is life just a big bunch of craziness all the time? Where is the plan and pattern to all that happens around us?

Well, just like Delbert and his buddies were baffled by the strange tracks in the snow and the sight of a horse sliding down the hill on her back, we can wonder what God is up to.

Once they saw Skookum's plan, it made perfect sense. People love sledding down a snowy hill, so did Skookum. Her actions weren't as crazy as they seemed.

Trust that the Lord has a plan. That while what he is doing might be different than you expected, it is a plan that comes out of his great love and strength. He is able to make a pathway through the wilderness and provide water in a dry land. He can make sense out of the crazy things around us and cause something amazing to blossom in our difficult and crazy world.

Dear Lord,

Sometimes the things around me are so baffling. Please help me to trust that your plan is good. Please help me to remember that you are a God of gentleness, power, and love who wants the best for his children.

Amen.

31

BREAKING TRAIL WITH CAPTAIN

"Some nations boast of their chariots and horses,
but we boast in the name of the Lord our God."
Psalm 20:7

B ack in the 1960s, in the deep of winter, there were only two ways to travel up into the mountain meadow where our family lives now. Since no one plowed the snow off the twisty logging roads that accessed this lovely refuge, folks could only get there on a snowmobile or a horse.

Before they started Camas Meadows Bible Camp, Del and Autumn enjoyed visiting the meadow where Autumn's sister Lily made her home. So that visits could occur more easily, Grandpa Del would get Lily's big horse, Captain, and plow the roads. Del didn't actually own a plow. What he did instead was hitch a wedge made from boards behind this powerful animal and drag it to push the heavy snow aside.

One time, the family got snowed in while they were up on the meadow. The snow was too deep for their snowmobiles and so the only way to make it down the mountain and back to civilization was to ride Captain. He was a tall and powerful horse, half thoroughbred and half Morgan. Captain broke through the deep snow at the front of the line and all the other horses followed behind in the path he'd made.

Horses are amazing animals and incredibly strong. Now days, we use a plow truck with a roaring engine and lots of power to clear the road. But it is so important not to rely on a powerful horse or a roaring plow truck for security.

Are there things around you that make you feel safe? Good! We can be thankful for everything God provides, but I do want you to remember something important. It is not in the strength of a horse, the power of a plow truck, a warm house with strong walls, or parents who make plenty of money that we should trust to keep us safe in the storm. Maybe it is a real storm, rattling windows and piling up snow outside your window. Maybe it is something that just feels like a storm because it makes your heart ache, like a friendship that is difficult or a person you love getting sick or a special pet who dies.

In that storm, trust in the strength of God. We can pile strong things around us, like people who look out for us, reliable cars, good winter clothes, or the emergency kit we keep with bandages and medicine. But those things are not as strong as our God. Trust in his love and his power. He is good and he loves you more than you can ever imagine.

Dear Lord,

When I want to surround myself with strong things to protect me and hide in a safe place from the hard stuff, please help me to trust in your strength. Remind me of your love, reach your strong hand out to rescue me, and help me to trust in you.

Amen.

32

SUNDANCE AND THE TREES

"Jesus told him, 'I am the way, the truth, and the life. No one can come to the Father except through me.'"

John 14:6

Before Grandpa Del bought him from a lady in Wenatchee, Sundance had been a stable horse all his life. His registered name was Shahzada, and he was a prancing, snorting, gorgeous dapple gray with a lot of spirit and smarts.

However, he had never encountered a forest.

When Autumn and Delbert brought him up to the meadow, they put Sundance in the fenced corral next to Lily's barn. He understood corrals. All was well as long as he was in the corral. But eventually, they let him out into the big pasture, which included both a mountain meadow and a thickly forested hillside.

Sundance was horrified.

All the other horses were running through the meadow, which he was brilliant at of course, but then they just melted into the trees and were gone. It was like magic. Horses in the meadow . . . horses go into the trees and suddenly disappear! Had the forest eaten them?!?

Sundance ran back and forth along the tree line, snorting and whinnying and calling for his new friends to come back.

Sundance had no idea that the tall brown trunks were not an impenetrable fence barring him from the other horses and whatever fun they were having on the hillside beyond. He didn't know that he had exactly what was needed to walk into that forest himself and join them. Four hooves and a head on his shoulders.

Now, he eventually figured it out. In fact, I recall one ride on Sundance when I was a girl where he bolted after smelling something that alarmed him. Boy did we run through trees, and fast!

Sometimes, we can be just like Sundance. Running back and forth at the edge of the trees.

We have everything we need to reach God, a loving father who longs for us to come to him. Jesus has died for every single sin we have ever done and every sin we will ever do. We can belong to God because Jesus made the way.

But sometimes it feels like we have to perform a magic trick to make that happen, melt into the trees and disappear like Sundance thought the other horses had done.

No, you have all that you need. Reach out to Jesus, he has made your path clear. You don't have to whinny and snort—just take that first step beyond the meadow and know that you are free.

Dear Lord,

Please help me when I am acting like Sundance, afraid to step into the trees when I have exactly what you gave me to make it through. I want to trust you with each day I have and know that you made life with God possible for me. Thank you for your love and sacrifice.

Amen.

33

THE HORSE THIEF

"Don't let your hearts be troubled. Trust in God, and trust also in me. There is more than enough room in my Father's home. If this were not so, would I have told you that I am going to prepare a place for you? When everything is ready, I will come and get you, so that you will always be with me where I am."

John 14:1-3

Sundance was known to steal things. Not because he wanted those things, but because he liked to investigate new items and tote stuff around. He enjoyed the pure pleasure of having made off with an item that his people wanted.

A painter friend of my grandparents asked permission to set up his easel and paint the lovely meadow where we now live. He had everything set up and was ready to begin when a huge creature snuck up behind him and started breathing down his neck while he attempted to work.

Sundance had jumped the fence!

The spirited gray horse nosed the artist with his muzzle, nibbled at the back of his neck while he worked, and then noticed the paint tubes. Sundance nudged around with his lips until he picked up the paint tubes. He then ran off with them and squeezed the paint out of the tubes and all over the ground.

The artist grabbed his halter and led Sundance back to the corral. He locked the gate carefully, then he settled back down to work.

A long nose reached over his shoulder. A velvety lip nudged at his brushes. Sundance picked up another tube of paint and pranced around with his new toy.

Every time the painter put him back, Sundance simply jumped the fence and then leaned over his shoulder to "help." The artist finally stormed away, thwarted by the antics of a single curious horse.

One time, Grandpa Del lost his favorite chainsaw. He'd set it down on top of one of the fence posts by the horse corral. Later, he spotted Sundance, carrying the chainsaw around by the handle. Sundance was a horse thief!

When Del, Autumn, and Aunt Lily were out building fences, Sundance was right there. He'd steal their bag of nails and run off with them, prancing and hoping to play a rousing game of keep away!

Are you worried about the things you love being taken away?

Maybe it's not art supplies or a chainsaw, but there might be something you care a lot about and you wonder if it is truly safe.

Not only does Jesus promise in Matthew 6:20 that moths and rust will not destroy our stuff in Heaven, but in John 14:1-3 he tells us that he is preparing a place just for us and there will be plenty of room for God's children to live there forever with him! We will not have to fret and worry about if there is enough, Jesus himself has prepared a place for us. We can trust that it will be exactly what we need. In Heaven, no matter how many pesky horses are trotting about, thieves won't be able to steal what we love and there will be plenty of space for everyone who answers God's call. Heaven is paradise and we can trust that we will be safe and cared for there with Jesus as our King.

Dear Lord,

Please help me to trust my concerns and all my things to you and to put my hope in the beauty of Heaven, knowing that you will take good care of all your children in your kingdom.

Amen.

34

FOOLISHNESS AND A DANGER TO ALL

"The wise are glad to be instructed,
but babbling fools fall flat on their faces."
Proverbs 10:8

On a quiet walk with their dogs, my grandma Autumn and great aunt Lily didn't pause to consider how obedient their pups were. Their dogs obeyed well enough for bounding down the dirt road that wound through the forest, sniffing after flowers and birds, and darting after squirrels.

After some delightful sniffing and wagging and good clean fun, the dogs discovered something amazing.

A black bear!

They took off after the bear, barking ferociously. Autumn and Lily were horrified. The bear was a much better fighter and was so much larger than their poor pups. The dogs' fun was actually very dangerous, but the foolish animals didn't know it.

With stern voices, they called the dogs back.

Bark! Bark! Bark!

Chase, zip, nip!

Now, black bears will almost always leave you alone. However, they will make an exception if you run up and bite them!

Even though the bear had been trundling along, minding his own business, those dogs were determined to fight that bear and win. They did not. With one mighty paw, the bear swatted one of the dogs and he went rolling like a beach ball. Dazed, the dog shook his head and slowly got back to his feet. The bear didn't fight like a dog at all. What had they gotten themselves into?

At this point, the dogs decided that it was time to obey. Time to run back to their owners who were still standing in the road yelling. So those dogs took off back to their people, lickety-split.

The bear followed those naughty dogs at a rolling, rumbling gallop.

Grandma Autumn and Great Aunt Lily looked at each other. They'd called for dogs and got dogs. But now the bear was coming, too!

They immediately started shouting for their dogs to go away!

Thankfully, the bear just wanted to give the dogs a chase and a bit of a scare. Once all those pesky canines were heading away, the bear was happy to leave them alone.

Have you ever wondered why God asks us to obey him? God's instructions can seem unnecessary. But just like those dogs must have thought a shout from their owners was just a foolish interruption to their fun, we don't always see everything that is going on. My grandmother and great aunt knew a thing or two about bears that those dogs did not.

It was because of Autumn and Lily's concern and love for their dogs that they called them away from the bear. It is because of God's great love for you and me that he asks us to obey as well. Don't be like a barking dog charging after a bear. Pause a moment to listen for the voice of your master.

Dear Lord,

Sometimes it feels like you want me to obey for no reason at all. Please help me to remember that you see everything that is going on all around me and know what will help and what will hurt. Please remind me to trust in your great love.

Amen.

35

THE CAT NAMED STUPID

"But most of all, my brothers and sisters, never take an oath, by heaven or earth or anything else. Just say a simple yes or no, so that you will not sin and be condemned."
James 5:12

My great uncle Jack (the same Jack who shot his cousin playing quick draw) thought it would be hilarious to name his cat Stupid. I'm not sure if he hadn't really wanted a cat in the first place, if he had known too many cats who scratched when he was younger, or if he just had a strange sense of humor. Whatever the reason, he did indeed name his cat Stupid.

The problem was, he really cared about that cat. The name he gave didn't reflect how he felt about his pet. It wasn't a very truthful name and eventually it got him into trouble.

Now, some time later, Stupid ran away.

Uncle Jack faced a terrible fate. He had to make a choice. Either not look for his cat . . . or walk around town calling out, "Here, Stupid! Here, Stupid, Stupid, Stupid!"

As I said, he really liked his cat and so off Uncle Jack went, calling and shouting for Stupid all over the neighborhood. Don't worry, Stupid was found, but Uncle Jack had the chance to seriously consider and reconsider his choice of names.

Have you ever said something that wasn't really true? Did it catch up to you like Uncle Jack's strange cat name?

This is why God calls us to simply say yes and no and mean what we say. The truth is an incredibly valuable thing and if my great uncle Jack had been just a bit more honest about how he truly felt about his cat, it would have saved him a whole lot of strange looks as he walked around town calling out, "Here, Stupid!"

Dear Lord,

Please help me find truthful words to say when I'm tempted to make something appear differently than it actually is. Give me your love for the truth and the bravery to live honestly.

Amen.

PART 4

GREG'S STORIES

Gregory Lee Griffith was my dad and the son of Del and Autumn. He grew up in Chelan, Washington before they started Camas Meadows Bible Camp and had many adventures there with his two brothers and sister. He was a pastor, a prankster, and eventually the camp's first director. He was also an amazing storyteller. He could silence a room with a single word and hold the attention of the whole camp with only a story to aid him. So grab your squeaky rat (yes, he had one), your favorite dog, and your Bible and get ready for a tale.

36

DIVING UNDER THE DOCK

"Don't be fooled by those who say such things, for 'bad company corrupts good character.'"
1 Corinthians 15:33

My dad, Greg, grew up a block from Lake Chelan. He spent much of his childhood and teen years swimming in one of the cleanest, most beautiful lakes in the world.

Greg had a dog named Stubbs. Stubbs was half Airedale and half Irish setter, had a stubbed tail, and loved his family very very much. So much that he would follow them anywhere.

Well, one time Greg was out swimming in Lake Chelan and he and his friends were diving underwater and coming up underneath the floating dock. There is a pocket of air under a dock and so they just hung out there for a time while Stubbs tried to find them. Then they would pop back out and say "hi" to the searching pup. Poor Stubbs was so confused. Where had they gone?

However, Stubbs was a smart dog and he figured it out.

He dove underwater and appeared beside Greg in the air pocket under the dock. Yay! Stubbs got to hang out with his boys.

Except, Stubbs didn't know how to get back out from under the dock.

He was stuck.

Stubbs had followed his boys and learned their behavior, but it led to him being trapped underneath the dock, swimming back and forth and wondering how he was ever going to be free again.

Greg had to help Stubbs. This involved some activities that Stubbs was not fond of. Greg pressed Stubbs underneath the water so that he would dive once more and then dragged him out from under the dock. But Greg had to do it to get his big doggy back to shore where he belonged.

Have you ever copied what someone else was doing and then regretted it, just like poor Stubbs?

The Bible says that who your friends are matters because if they are being foolish, you might begin to act foolishly as well. Their bad behavior can start to change you so that you begin to behave badly, too. Be very careful who you imitate. Be the one to guide others toward honoring God with what you do, not the one who copies everything you see.

Be even smarter than Stubbs, don't follow the boys and doggy paddle under the dock!

Dear Lord,

Please help me to notice when my friends are leading me into actions that don't please you. Help me to be someone who loves your ways and who makes those around me want to do the right things and live a life of love.

Amen.

37

THE GIANT BOUNCY WHEEL

"For if you listen to the word and don't obey, it is like glancing at your face in a mirror. You see yourself, walk away, and forget what you look like."

James 1:23-24

L ake Chelan is surrounded by tall desert hills, one of which is called "The Butte."

When my dad was a boy, he spent many hours wandering The Butte. Its sage-filled heights offered a host of adventures. There were old homesteads complete with gravestones and even the occasional scorpion skittering across the rocky ground. Then there was that amazing day that he found the giant bouncy wheel.

Greg and at least one buddy (and perhaps a brother or two) were up on The Butte and they came across the ruins of an old wagon. Part of this abandoned heap was a giant wheel. All the wooden parts had rotted away, leaving behind a huge band of metal.

This metal wheel rim was sprongy and amazing!

It was at this point, that Greg had a "brilliant" idea. What if they sent this giant metal rim bouncing down the twisty road all the way to the bottom of The Butte?

Now, Greg was very briefly concerned that such a journey might end with the metal rim landing on a car.

To avoid this, the boys peered down the twisty road, waiting to see if the way was clear.

It looked good!

One, two, three!

They let the huge metal rim go.

A car appeared at that very moment, at the very bottom of the road.

The wheel bounced in huge leaps down the road toward the unsuspecting vehicle. *Boing, boing, boing!* The boys watched in horror. What had they unleashed? The car drove up curve after curve in the road, up, up, up.

The wheel bounded down.

The car chugged closer.

Farther down the road bounced the wheel.

Dad and his buddies were biting their fingernails, wondering how much trouble would occur if that wheel hit the car. Would the car be dented, or crash? Would the driver be injured? What would their parents say?

Closer and closer the two objects traveled.

The car whipped around a corner as the wheel bounced its way. The wheel took one more bounce and landed directly in front of the car. With a great and powerful sprong, it leaped right over the car and continued on its way down The Butte.

Greg and his friends sagged with relief.

He'd known that releasing that wheel was a risk, but didn't think anything would actually happen. Who would have guessed a car would appear right then?

Well, anyone who looked closely at the road might imagine a car driving up it. Greg knew what the smart thing was . . . but didn't do it.

The Bible says that when we listen to God's word but don't do what it says, we are like someone who looks at their face in a mirror and then forgets what they look like.

Or . . . like someone who looks at a road and forgets that a car could be driving on it so they bounce a giant wheel right on down The Butte!

Dear Lord,

Help me to both listen to and do the things you want for me. Help me to become someone who obeys you. Please remind me of the dangers of ignoring your words, like a giant wheel bouncing down the road. Thank you for your wise words and your love.

Amen.

38

STUBBS GOES WATERSKIING

"Then the angel of the LORD came again and touched him and said, 'Get up and eat some more, or the journey ahead will be too much for you.'"
I Kings 19:7

My dad, Greg, bought a boat before he bought his first car. Because he lived a block away from Lake Chelan, the teens he hung out with drove boats more often than cars.

He loved to waterski, but Greg had a very special dog named Stubbs who followed him everywhere. Stubbs did not know how to waterski; however, Stubbs didn't realize this.

Wanting to go skiing with friends, Greg left Stubbs home. Unknown to him, his dog escaped. Greg was standing on the end of the dock in his skis, holding the rope. His friends were in the boat, about to take off. They waited for the signal to gun the engine sending Greg zipping off the dock and across the water. Greg gave the signal. The engine revved.

At that point, Greg looked back.

There was Stubbs, running full tilt towards him, missing his person! Greg turned to tell the driver to stop, but it was too late.

The boat zipped forward, Greg shot off the dock, landed on the lake, and skimmed across the water. Stubbs saw him go.

Instead of heading back home. Stubbs knew what to do. He would catch his favorite person! So, Stubbs ran to the end of the dock, leaped off, and started paddling as hard as he could after Greg.

By the time Greg signaled wildly enough to get the boat stopped and turned around, Stubbs was nowhere to be seen. He was swimming, somewhere in the center of the lake. Now Lake Chelan is enormous. It is not an easy swim across and though they searched and searched, no one could find the missing dog.

Greg despaired of ever finding Stubbs again. At some point, the strong and loyal beast would tire and the chase would become too much for him. Greg's chest squeezed as he thought about his dog sinking into the depths of Lake Chelan.

Much later, after everyone had given up, Stubbs dragged himself from the water. Sides heaving with exhaustion, Stubbs stumbled home. Poor boy. Who knows how far he swam looking for his person. The task was too hard for him. He wasn't a water-skier.

Sometimes we face a task that is much too big. Like Elijah who needed to eat and rest before his long journey.

If you are trying to do a task that feels too big, stop and ask yourself if maybe you should be praying and asking for help. Is it something you can't change? Give it over to God. Is it something a friend can help you with? Two people working often make a task easier. God has put other people in our lives so that we don't have to face life alone. Don't forget that while some things are too big for us, God is never too powerful and mighty to be concerned for his children.

Ask God to help you in the hard things, he knows when you are tired and need new strength.

Dear Lord,

Please help me to see when something is too big for me to handle. Just like when you helped Elijah and sent an angel with a snack, please help me. Give me strength to hand the things I can't control over to you, to ask for help from a friend, and to try my best with the things that I have the power to change.

Amen.

39

STUBBS SNIFFS OUT DANGER

"In his grace, God has given us different gifts for doing certain things well. So if God has given you the ability to prophesy, speak out with as much faith as God has given you. If your gift is serving others, serve them well. If you are a teacher, teach well. If your gift is to encourage others, be encouraging. If it is giving, give generously. If God has given you leadership ability, take the responsibility seriously. And if you have a gift for showing kindness to others, do it gladly."

Romans 12:6-8

My dad's dog Stubbs loved kids and he loved visitors at all hours day or night. Stubbs was used to having random teenagers sleep over in his yard and enjoyed camping out with them under the stars.

One warm summer morning, the yard was scattered with local teens in sleeping bags. No one was quite awake yet. No one but Stubbs, who was watching over all the kids under his charge.

Suddenly, someone new approached.

This new person vaulted over the fence and ran through the yard. Stubbs took off like a shot. He ran, he barked, he backed that stranger up against the fence and wouldn't let him leave.

Grandma Autumn rushed out of the house in a tizzy. How embarrassing. Stubbs had never behaved this way before. What a bad dog.

The police pulled up to the yard. They'd been searching for this very person. He had been involved in a knife fight and was fleeing the scene. Although Stubbs had never growled and barked at anyone before, he decided to capture this man. The very man the police had been looking for.

God gave Stubbs special wisdom about that man. Dogs can smell certain scents on a person when they are running from others. Officers will train dogs to pick up these scents but Stubbs didn't need training. He used the gifts God had given him right there in his snout to protect his kids as they slept on the lawn.

What gifts has God given you?

You probably can't sniff out danger, but can you spot someone who is having a hard day, who really needs a friend? Do you have great ideas for fun projects to do outside? Do you play music, a sport, or draw amazing pictures? Can you memorize long Bible verses or do tricky math problems? Are you able to tell stories and read large books? Can you cheer up a friend when they are down or cook soft and gooey cookies? God has gifted you. Be like Stubbs! Use your gifts wisely, to honor God and to show his love and care to everyone around you.

Dear Lord,

Sometimes I feel very ordinary. Sometimes I feel like the things I do don't matter. Please show me the gifts you have given me and teach me to use them well. Just like Stubbs used his nose to protect his family, help me to notice the ways you have made me and to use my gifts to show love and encourage others. Thank you for the gifts you give.

Amen.

40

STUBBS AND THE SCATTERED BUNNIES

"But the Holy Spirit produces this kind of fruit in our lives: love, joy, peace, patience, kindness, goodness, faithfulness, gentleness, and self-control. There is no law against these things!"
Galatians 5:22-23

My dad's dog Stubbs was smart and fast, but he was also incredibly gentle. When Greg was growing up, their neighbor had bunnies.

Now, these bunnies would sometimes escape. If you have ever tried to catch a bunny, you can appreciate the difficulty that these escaping rabbits gave the neighbors. The neighbors also had a dog. A dog who was smart and fast. Smart and fast enough to catch bunnies. But their dog was not gentle and could not control his drive to hunt and kill.

Stubbs was both gentle and self-controlled.

So, when the neighbor's bunnies escaped, they knew just what to do. They put their own dog inside and then came over to my dad's house and asked to borrow Stubbs.

Stubbs was happy to help.

He went with Greg over to the neighbor's yard and hunted bunnies. Stubbs used his smarts and speed to capture each bunny. Then he used his self-control to stop himself from killing the escaped rabbit. With gentle paws, he would hold the bunny down until Greg came to collect the escaped critter. Greg would give the frightened rabbit to its owner, captured, but unharmed.

Did you know that gentleness and self-control are fruits of God's Spirit? They are a part of God's character and he wants to see us becoming more like him by growing our own gentleness and self-control.

If Stubbs hadn't had gentleness and self-control, those bunnies would have been in trouble. We can be like our gentle and self-controlled God. As we grow more and more like him, we can love and help others, too.

Dear Lord,

Thank you that you are gentle and self-controlled. That you do not crush us with your mighty power but use all things to work together for good. I thank you for Stubbs, a good dog who could gently capture bunnies without doing them harm. A good dog who shows me what you are like. Lord, teach me how to use gentleness and self-control to show your love to each person I see today.

Amen.

41

GREG AND THE UGLY BABY

"How much better to get wisdom than gold,
and good judgment than silver!"
Proverbs 16:16

There is a difference between truth and wisdom. The Bible talks a lot about wisdom, especially in the book of Proverbs. When I read through the book of Proverbs, I often think about my dad, Greg. He loved to quote the book of Proverbs. The weirder the verse, the better! As a little girl, I heard his favorites often.

"As a dog returns to its vomit,
so a fool repeats his foolishness."
Proverbs 26:11 (NLT)
"The lazy person claims, 'There's a lion on the road!
Yes, I'm sure there's a lion out there!'"
Proverbs 26:13 (NLT)
"Even fools are thought wise when they keep silent;
with their mouths shut, they seem intelligent."
Proverbs 17:28 (NLT)

My dad was certainly not a foolish person, but he did love to laugh. There were times when chasing a joke got him into trouble. Like when he asked my mother to be the Sasquatch for a game at the camp we work at. While Mom was getting into the furry suit and putting on a gorilla mask, Dad explained to the campers that they wouldn't get all the possible points for their cabin by capturing the Sasquatch if they didn't lead the mighty beast back to camp properly. What is the proper way to lead a Sasquatch? By putting your fingers in its nose and leading it along! My mother was not amused when her capturing camper put their fingers in her monkey mask nose to lead her back to the main lodge!

Before he was a camp director, Dad was a pastor. He still had that odd sense of humor, too. While Greg adored his own children and was happy to meet the babies of others, it was his opinion that all babies were ugly. He felt that they greatly improved with age and thought it was funny that folks felt obligated to say "My, what a beautiful baby!" whenever photos of infants were brought out.

After admiring several babies in close succession and saying what he felt were white lies (the babies were wrinkly and red) Dad felt that it would be incredibly funny to be boldly truthful. He was a pastor after all. Pastors were supposed to tell the truth! When the head of the mission he worked for pulled out photos of his newest grandchild, Dad felt that his moment for hilarious honesty had come.

"Wow! What an ugly baby!" he exclaimed.

Silence.

The mission director did not laugh.

Greg's chuckle faded.

The mission director put away his photos in utter silence.

My dad realized something important that day. There is a reason that God urges us to pursue wisdom, not just blatant truth. Bare truth can actually cause harm, even though the words may be true. God wants us to say the truth, but in love (Ephesians 4:15). Wisdom understands that the beauty of a baby encompasses more than hair, skin, and eyes. A tiny piece of humanity in your arms, part of Mom and part of Dad and all their own person, too. A miracle that is not made less beautiful just because babies tend to be wrinkly and red. Wisdom sees the beauty in that tiny scrunched up face and rejoices along with their family.

Dear Lord,

Please help me to remember that wisdom is important as well as truth. Give me a heart to serve others and when it is time to speak the truth, give me the ability to do it in love.

Amen.

PART 5

KRISTEN AND DARYL'S STORIES

As you may have guessed, I am Kristen Joy Wilks, daughter of Greg Griffith and Judy Dewsnap and wife to Camas Meadows Bible Camp's current camp director Daryl "Scruffy" Wilks. I grew up first on a farm in the tiny community of Wishkah, Washington and then "up on the meadow" where our family lived with Del and Autumn in their log home. After I moved away for college, the camp hired my boyfriend as their program director. After we married, Scruff became the camp director and we raised our three sons (and various dogs and chickens) "up on the meadow" as well. So grab your pet chicken, saddle up that angry pony, and get ready for the next generation of rough and rowdy tales.

42

THE DARE TO DARE

*"You must not follow the crowd in doing wrong. When you
are called to testify in a dispute, do not be swayed by the
crowd to twist justice."*
Exodus 23:2

When I was about five years old, we lived on a cow
farm because that was where the parsonage was.
My dad was a pastor in a small rural community and the
parsonage was an old farmhouse next to the vast cow pastures of a local farmer.

Well, the farmer's daughter was a force to be reckoned with. Often, I was baffled by her ways and totally unprepared to avoid her tomfoolery.

One time, we were hanging on the fence looking at one of the bulls. He'd been separated from the herd and was in a small corral next to a large stone barn.

The farmer's daughter gazed across the pen at that bull. "Kristen, I dare you to run across the bull pen, tag the stone barn, and run back."

But I was ready for this kind of foolishness. "No," I said.

She was not undone. "Kristen, I dare you to dare me to run across the bull pen, tag the stone barn, and run back."

"N—"

"I accept!"

She jumped over the fence and took off like a shot!

The bull was amazed. Frozen in place from his spot across the bull pen, that bull just stared.

Boom, she tagged the barn.

The bull was baffled.

Back across the bull pen like a streak of lighting with black hair flying and a reckless gleam in her eye, she ran. The farmer's daughter hopped back over the fence, panting, "I did it!"

Even at five years old, I knew that if she'd been gored by the bull—and lived—the farmer's daughter would have told her parents, "Kristen dared me to do it!" I was very pleased that the bull had been just as baffled by her behavior as I'd been. For more reasons than one!

Thankfully, no one was hurt, but I learned my lesson well. Following the crowd is dangerous in so many ways. Like the Bible verse above says, it is dangerous for justice, for others who need us to be strong and take a stand. But when running across bull pens is concerned, following the crowd was also dangerous for my safety and the safety of those around me.

Also, be very careful around friends who are full of tomfoolery. Keep an eye out for their traps and tricks and always stay on the correct side of the bull pen.

Dear Lord,

Help me to be wise and not blindly follow what people say. Give me wisdom with people who have tricksy ways and help me to always seek you as I make choices each day.

Amen.

43

PRAYING FOR A PONY AGAINST MY PARENTS' WISHES

"I pray that God, the source of hope, will fill you complete-ly with joy and peace because you trust in him. Then you will overflow with confident hope through the power of the Holy Spirit."
Romans 15:13

When I was three years old, the only thing I wanted in all the world was my very own pony. While perhaps every little girl has wanted a pony at some point, my passion was especially strong.

You see, my dad was a pastor, and I had learned all about prayer. Every night when my parents tucked me into bed beside my stuffed animals, they asked what I would like to pray about.

I prayed that God would give me a pony!

I prayed this prayer every single night, for a year. I still remember my mother gently trying to encourage other kinds of prayers. Nope, although I was now a mature four-year-old, I still knew God was able to give me a pony and so I boldly asked for one. Why ask for something else, when what I really wanted was a pony?

She attempted to introduce the idea that God might choose not to give me a pony. Well, it didn't hurt to ask and He was God! A pony would not be a problem.

After their attempts to steer my young faith in non-pony directions, my parents considered the possibility of a pony for Christmas. They were not wealthy and ponies were pricy animals to acquire. They searched for a bargain pony and peered at our small backyard, wondering if there was any way to cram a pony inside. After much praying and counting of pennies they came to the sad conclusion that they could not get me a pony. They approached Christmas with troubled hearts. Would I be able to let go of my pony dreams to enjoy the day?

Then, something strange and amazing occurred.

Out of the blue, someone gave them a pony.

Boom! Just like that.

They stood aghast. A pony. Free. For their fiercely praying daughter. A pony straight from God. God decided to say "yes" even after their careful calculations and conclusions that it wasn't possible.

Shortcake was an angry circus pony with a chip on her shoulder and enough grit and pizzaz for ten ponies combined. She was my treasure. Shortcake loved to buck, bite, escape the corral, and drink root beer out of the can. She was a gift directly from God. Shortcake's appearance was my first glimpse of how very much God loves us, every day, all the time.

Since then, God has answered "no" to plenty of my prayers. Whenever he says "no" I am still able to walk beside him through whatever path he is asking me to take. For this is the same God who gives ponies to little girls against their parents' wishes. His love is that of a gracious and giving father, whatever the sorrow or joy.

God loves you just as much! The God who gives ponies wants to give you every good thing. We may not know what that looks like, but we can trust that he does and will be with us in the ups and downs. Will you take his hand and trust?

Dear Lord,

You don't always say "yes" to my prayers and it is easy to feel discouraged. Help me to remember the great things you have done. The ponies and the joy. Remind me of your tender love for me and help me to trust you today.

Amen.

44

DANGLED OVER THE SNAKE PIT

"Then Jesus said to the crowds and to his disciples,
'The teachers of religious law and the Pharisees are the of-
ficial interpreters of the law of Moses. So practice and obey
whatever they tell you, but don't follow their example. For
they don't practice what they teach.'"
Matthew 23:1-3

When I was a girl, we watched a movie about an archeologist who wielded a bullwhip and didn't like snakes. After watching him and his heroine dangling over a snake pit, we came to the obvious conclusion. We needed a snake pit of our very own!

Inspired by this movie legend, my brother, two cousins, and I began to dig. Now, we lived at Camas Meadows Bible Camp in Eastern Washington and the hard-packed dirt is about as hard as concrete in the summer. Digging that snake pit took a long time, but we were wildly dedicated. Eventually, we finally finished a pit that was about four feet deep.

Now, we needed snakes!

Thankfully, there are no venomous snakes in our area and so the whole group of us set out for the meadow and the pond, where most of the snakes hang out. It took all day, but with four children dedicated to the task, we captured twenty-one startled serpents.

Then for the grand finale! We moved the twenty-one snakes into our brand-new pit. Then we built a tripod over our pit out of three logs and baling twine. Finally, we tied another length of baling twine so that it was dangling down from the log tripod.

Since I was the oldest, I demanded the honor of being the damsel in distress.

I did a handstand, and my helpful relations tied my feet with the baling twine. We made the moment dramatic with a few "terrified" screams from me while the rest of the children acted all villainous. Upside down, with my feet secured to the log tripod, they pushed me out over the snake pit.

We discovered something unfortunate.

It is much scarier for the dangling heroine to *almost* touch the snakes. There is a sense of drama there. But I was too tall and my head plopped in the dirt at the bottom of our pit. Therefore, the snakes just crawled around in my hair doing nothing. I was unharmed by our wonderful collection of serpents, and it was really boring. So, I lost the position of honor and my shorter cousin became the damsel.

My cousin dangled several inches above the snakes and screamed. It was super scary and pretty amazing! Operation Snake Pit was a complete success!

Now, some of you may have noticed how greatly influenced we were by watching a single movie. Thankfully, not so influenced that we wanted venomous snakes, but influenced all the same. Jesus warns about imitating the wrong people. We want to grow to be more like him and that means letting folks influence us who are also trying to be like Jesus, especially in the way they treat others.

Think of how much power that movie had over us. We dug all summer long. We spent an entire day catching snakes. We dangled two different people over our snake pit until we achieved just the right level of drama!

Be cautious about who you want to be like. There are movies, songs, games, and real people out there who are doing stuff that's a lot more dangerous than dangling over a pit of harmless snakes.

Dear Lord,

Please give me wisdom to know when something is influencing me. Please give me a heart that longs to become more like you.

Amen.

45

SUNDANCE AND THE SCARY BUSH

"Trust in the LORD with all your heart;
do not depend on your own understanding. Seek his will
in all you do,
and he will show you which path to take."
Proverbs 3:5-6

My horse, Sundance, acted like he was afraid of everything. Down deep, he was actually a really solid horse.

Later, we were given another horse named Gypsy. She acted slow and calm, but if something truly frightened her, watch out!

When I rode Sundance, he would prance, snort, and shy sideways upon encountering everyday things. A scary bush, a brisk wind whipping through the trees, a suspicious stump . . . However, he wasn't genuinely afraid. Sundance was just having fun. I could ride Sundance anywhere. Grandpa Del even treed a bear while on Sundance. Treeing a bear is where dogs (or in rare cases, horses) chase a bear until it runs up a tree. When I needed him, Sundance was as brave as anyone and I could count on him to keep his head in tight spots.

When I rode Gypsy, she just plodded along. She didn't prance, snort, or shy. She walked and she walked slowly.

One day I was riding her deep in the woods and Gypsy smelled something that truly scared her. It was most likely a black bear or a cougar. We have both in the woods and meadows where I live.

When Sundance would smell a bear or cougar, he'd get up on his toes, prancing and snorting and making a big fuss, but I could always calm him down because he wasn't really scared. He trusted me.

Whatever Gypsy smelled turned her inside out.

She reared up higher and higher until I was afraid she would go over backwards. Gypsy dumped me off her back and then bolted straight back to the barn, faster than I'd ever seen her run before.

So there I was, abandoned by my horse, alone in the woods. I had to walk back, wondering which of our forest predators had sent my horse running and if they were still nearby.

Sundance would never have left me in such a spot. His snorts and sidesteps were a warning and part of the fun of riding, but he always listened if I kept a firm hand on the reins.

Sundance and I trusted each other and had a partnership when we rode.

Gypsy was terrified and unwilling to trust me to get her home in one piece.

Which horse are you like when God asks you to walk through a difficult situation? I understand Gypsy. Dumping the rider on her back and running made sense to her. So, she did just that. But this left Gypsy without the care and guidance that a rider provides. Bears and cougars are afraid of humans. They are not afraid of horses.

Sundance knew that we were safer riding together and trusted me to guide him home.

Don't let your fear send you running off without talking to God. Whatever way he is asking you to go, you can trust that it is the best way for you. God sometimes asks us to walk a scary path, but he is with us all the while. We are safer on the scary path with God than on the easy-looking path alone.

Dear Lord,

When I face scary things, please remind me that I am safer going the way you ask than going my own way. Remind me of your power and love, how you care for each of your children, and that even the darkest path is light to you. Help me to walk in trust as I follow your ways.

Amen.

46

KRISTEN'S HASTY GALLOP

"And let the peace that comes from Christ rule in your hearts. For as members of one body you are called to live in peace. And always be thankful."
Colossians 3:15

Our current herd of elk consists of about thirty to sixty animals. During my childhood, the meadow was home to a much larger herd of 200 elk. Now, cow elk can reach 600lbs and the bulls can top 1,000. They are wild creatures and best left alone. There is no need to be frightened of them, but elk do deserve a healthy dose of respect. While I enjoyed watching and photographing them, I didn't get too close.

Except for one time, when I was filled with fear for a friend.

I loved to go horseback riding with the neighbor girls. When I say neighbor, I mean the girls in the closest house to ours, which was about two miles away. We live in wild country full of forested hillsides that surround swaying meadow grasses. It is lovely. Normally a fun ride on our horses was enough to entertain. However, one of the neighbor girls was bored that day and decided that what she really wanted was to lasso an elk calf.

Despite elk being generally calm creatures, they are still large, wild, and unpredictable. As a rule, they are also opposed to being lassoed.

I expressed my concern.

She remained undaunted. My friend shook out her lasso—yes she just happened to bring it along—and kicked her horse Oliver right toward the herd of elk that was grazing out on the meadow.

I shouted for her return.

Nothing.

Desperate to stop my friend from a possible trampling, I kicked my horse Sundance into a run and rushed after her.

We galloped straight into the herd of 200 elk, splitting the herd. About 100 animals went to the right while the other 100 ran to the left.

Sundance and I were closing in on Oliver when my friend spotted a likely calf.

She tossed her lasso as I yelled for her to stop. The lasso bounced off the calf elk and momma elk noticed. With stern ears and bared teeth, she chased my friend and her horse away from the calf and out of the herd.

With a sigh of relief, I reined Sundance in. We fled the mess of milling elk and out of the meadow entirely.

Let the peace of Christ rule in your hearts . . .

I was so overwhelmed with concern for my friend, that I allowed fear to rule my heart. I convinced myself that I had to do something foolish. If I'd let the peace of Christ rule instead, I could have given my fear to the Lord, made a wiser decision, and not run Sundance straight into a herd of 200 wild animals. Turn to the Lord in prayer instead of giving your heart over to fear. His perfect love casts out fear and gives us the strength to trust.

Dear Lord,

It is hard to let your peace rule in my heart. My heart grabs onto worry so easily. Please remind me of the truths in your word and help me to seek your guidance when I'm in a situation that makes me afraid. Please give me the strength to accept your peace and let that direct my heart instead.

Amen.

47

BLIND TO THE COUGAR IN THE ROAD

"Then Jesus told him, 'You believe because you have seen me. Blessed are those who believe without seeing me.'"
John 20:29

When I was a teen, out riding horses with the neighbor girl, a cougar whispered across the road in front of us. He didn't hurry, but he was still fast. The cougar simply walked, quiet and deadly and strong.

We live in the territory of a female cougar, and he was coming to court her. He glanced our way and then dismissed us. It was like he didn't have the time or energy to bother with two teen girls out in his lady's forest for a ride. The horses didn't even twitch an ear. My friend and I slowly turned to look at each other, eyes wide.

"Did you see that?" we both said with hushed voices.

However, our horses remained oblivious. They were looking at the ground, the wind was blowing the scent of the cougar away, and while a dangerous predator prowled a few feet ahead, they didn't see a thing.

It was so strange that I waited a moment for him to move on and followed the cougar down a gulley and onto a side road, just to look for tracks. Yep, there in the mud was a giant cougar track. I measured it with my hand, amazed.

We know there is always a cougar around. We've talked to an old hunter who treed her with his dogs, just to catch a glimpse of her beauty. We know where she raises her kittens and that when she passes away, another lady cat will take her place. Her territory is the right size for a female and so another female will take over.

I've never seen her, though. I've lived within her territory for many years and I haven't seen her once. My sons have heard her scream in the night. Others have seen her big kittens out in the world, learning to run and hunt. I once saw her mate, coming to visit, but I've never actually seen the cougar in whose territory I reside. But I believe she is here, I know this truth deep down and she is no less powerful and real for my lack of a first-hand encounter.

When Jesus appeared to his disciples after raising from the dead, they believed. But Thomas wasn't there. When the others told him, Thomas's grief was so sharp that he boldly stated: *"I won't believe it unless I see the nail wounds in his hands, put my fingers into them, and place my hand into the wound in his side."*

Jesus appeared again, while Thomas was there. Christ simply showed Thomas His wounds and challenged him to believe. Then Jesus said something incredible about you and about me. *". . . Blessed are those who believe without seeing me."*

I didn't know Jesus when He walked this world, but in the same way I know I live in the territory of a cougar, I see the evidence of Jesus around me. Prayers answered. Hard hearts softened. Forgiveness offered. Lives changed. My own determined trudge toward destruction halted and my heart made clean and new. Look for the signs. He is here. You who believe are so very blessed!

Dear Lord,

Thank you for Thomas's story. He is such an encouragement to me. Thank you for leaving the message in scripture that you are thinking of us and are proud of those who put our faith in you.

Amen.

48

THE WRONG MIRACLE

"Now may the Lord of peace himself give you his peace at all times and in every situation. The Lord be with you all."

2 Thessalonians 3:16

When I was fourteen years old, God preformed a miracle for our family. It was a secret miracle that I only found out about much later and it was not the miracle I wanted. This miracle occurred right next to a staggering loss.

My Grandpa Dewsnap was a pastor. He was a quiet man who taught from God's word with a calm logic and soft-spoken passion that lacked dramatic showmanship but was full of gentle truth. After many years, he told my grandmother and his church that it was time to retire. What he didn't tell them was that he had received instructions from God.

Pick up and move. I want you to live near Judy. Someone close to her is going to die and she will need you both.

Judy is his daughter and my mother.

Grandpa Dewsnap thought about my Grandma Autumn, who had started the camp where we live and work with Grandpa Del and had a heart condition. Were we about to lose her? However, Grandpa Dewsnap didn't tell anyone what the Lord had said, not even Grandma Dewsnap. But he recognized the voice of his Lord and so he obeyed. They packed up and moved to Chelan, a seventy-minute drive from where we lived.

Some time later, my dad was working on a bank of batteries, part of the power system that brought electricity to our home. The generator was running and he thought it was sufficiently ventilated. However, a heavy snowfall blocked the exhaust from escaping. My dad died of accidental carbon monoxide poisoning when I was fourteen years old.

My mother and I did CPR out in the cold, trying to revive him. I prayed so desperately for Dad's healing. I prayed with confidence. This was the same God who had given me a Shetland pony against my parents' wishes. He could do this! I have no idea why, but God's answer was, no. However, God gave us the miracle we didn't want. Grandpa and Grandma Dewsnap had moved to live near us, because God told Grandpa Dewsnap that someone we needed was going to die.

It wasn't the miracle I wanted. My heart hurts knowing that God was aware of the terrible moment that would come. Doing chest compressions on my father for what seemed like forever while my mother did the breaths. Praying for Dad's return to us. Crying out to God.

Although God did not save my dad, he had quietly spoken into the ear of my Grandfather.

Someone close to her is going to die and she will need you both.

The Lord does offer peace, at all times. It is sometimes a hard peace, a difficult peace, but even in dark and terrible places, he is still there, caring for his children.

Dear Lord,

I don't want hard times. I want to rejoice over the prayers that you answer with a "yes." I want to feel protected from all the bad things in life. But if I must walk a hard path, please hold me close. Please remind me of your love and give me the strength to press forward on the journey you have asked me to make, whatever that looks like.

Amen.

49

A Dust Storm, the Dasher, and a Grumpy Granny

"The father instantly cried out, "I do believe, but help me overcome my unbelief!"
Mark 9:24

My husband was a poor college student when he found Jesus. His vehicle, a 1977 Volkswagen Dasher would die for four hours if he took his foot off the gas. Scruffy (that's his camp name) never turned his car off before parking for the night. Scruff carried a brick in his car. If he needed to go into a store, he pulled the parking brake and placed the brick on the gas pedal to keep the car running.

Now, Scruff is a skeptic. It was hard for him to believe God existed. It's a miracle he came to Christ at all, but once he did, he became a Christian who was a skeptic.

Scruff was driving the backroads of The Palouse, enormous stretches of farmland, with nothing else for miles. A severe dust storm kicked up, reducing visibility to near zero. Scruffy prayed as he drove, opening the car door to follow the yellow centerline. A drift of dust covered the centerline, and he drove off the road. The car got stuck and a tire came off the rim. The Dasher coughed and died. Dust started coming into the car.

Scruffy put a pillowcase over his head so he could breathe in the storm and set out looking for help.

Eventually, he spotted a farmhouse. Scruff stumbled onto the porch and knocked. After a long pause, a grandma lady cracked the door.

"Can I use your phone to call a tow truck?" he asked.

"No!" She slammed the door.

As dust swirled around him, Scruffy sat on the porch steps, praying.

A young mom pulled up. She dashed past Scruffy and knocked. The grandma lady opened the door. "Can I use your phone to call my husband?"

"Of course, Honey!"

Scruff probably looked terrifying. A tall young man with wild eyes and hair full of dirt.

Bedraggled and filthy, Scruff sat on the steps and continued to pray.

After her phone call, the mom returned to her car. She noticed Scruffy on the porch. "Do you want to come home with us?"

Yes, Scruffy did!

The young family brought him home that night. He played with their kids, ate homemade pizza with caribou sausage, and discovered they were followers of Jesus. Scruff realized that even if he'd been able to call a tow truck, they were all busy, for the storm had caused a huge ruckus. The next day, her husband (who owned a tow truck) towed Scruff's car, fixed the tire, and refused to take any money.

Scruff's adventure reminds me of Jesus and a skeptical father who wanted his son to be well, but wasn't sure how much believing his heart could handle. God wants us all and works with every kind of heart, drawing us toward himself.

Scruffy prayed for help. He is a skeptic, but prayed anyway. He drove through the storm. No miracle. He crashed and his car died. No miracle. He walked alone with a pillowcase over his head. No miracle. He found a farmhouse. No miracle. God was waiting and watching. God gave his servant the courage to invite a tall, dirty, stranger home. Scruffy was safe and well-loved that day. The miracle came. Despite Scruff's skeptical heart, he pressed on and God was there, waiting inside the storm.

Dear Lord,

Sometimes it is hard to believe, especially when I'm in a storm with a pillowcase over my head. Give me enough faith to continue through the storm, knowing you are there, and you love me.

Amen.

50

As Brave as a Chicken

"While Jesus was in the Temple, he watched the rich people dropping their gifts in the collection box. Then a poor widow came by and dropped in two small coins. 'I tell you the truth,' Jesus said, 'this poor widow has given more than all the rest of them. For they have given a tiny part of their surplus, but she, poor as she is, has given everything she has.'"

Luke 21:1-4

People say you are "chicken" when you're afraid and say "bird brained" when they mean unintelligent, but because of our sons' pet chickens we learned that these birds are much smarter and braver than is generally believed.

Our three sons each got pet chickens after Shamu, our first Newfoundland dog, died. Those three hens were so fun! They rode in the car, visited school, went on hikes with the boys to the meadow to chase grasshoppers and to the pond to eat bees, perched on bunk beds and in tree forts, and even went sledding. The chickens didn't particularly like sledding, but they rode down the icy hill with their boys all the same.

Chickens are smarter than people think. Paintball, our oldest son's hen, would run out to meet the car when I drove the boys home from the bus stop. She would even get upset if her boy held another chicken in his lap.

King, our middle son's hen, was the leader of the flock. Once, the door to their coop shut before the hens could get inside for the night. So King led our small flock to the window where they hopped up and perched until we came out to let them into their coop. That hen knew where the people lived and that we could fix her chicken coop troubles.

Once, I even witnessed Ewok, our youngest son's hen, have an epic battle with a squirrel. Ewok was a mad-hen! A roving squirrel decided he wanted to steal the chicken food. Well, Ewok would have none of it! The squirrel jumped onto Ewok's back and started biting and scratching and actually running in a loop around Ewok's neck.

I've seen squirrels run upside down on branches and even our porch railing, but until that fateful day, I had no idea that they could run upside down on a chicken! But Ewok didn't take this squirrel attack sitting down. Nope, she fought back! Ewok turned into a furious whirlwind of pecking, flapping, and scratching. And you know what? She won! Our own Ewok the chicken chased that bad squirrel away from the food and then all the hens ate in peace.

The way people misjudge chickens reminds me of something Jesus said to his disciples. They were all at the temple, watching some wealthy people giving huge amounts of money. Jesus directed the disciples' attention away from these flashy givers and pointed out the incredible value of a poor widow's gift.

Don't let the outside fool you. The people around you are amazing, surprising, and deeply loved by God! Who knows, you might be sitting in church next to a superstar. Someone like the widow Jesus watched, who humbly gave everything she had.

Dear Lord,

Please help me to see the incredible value of the people around me. How much you love them. What amazing abilities you've given them. Remind me of those smart and surprising chickens when I forget. Just like Paintball, King, and Ewok weren't "chicken" or "bird-brained" let me see the value of all the wonderful people you've made.

Amen.

Rosa's Sourdough Cinnamon Rolls

Grandpa Del told me about how his mother Rosa used to make sourdough rolls using a potato-based starter back in the 1920s. I researched online until I found several recipes that I liked and combined them to make this recipe which became a favorite both with Del and our three sons. Always remember what Grandpa Del told me, "Makes good cinnamon rolls, too."

*Begin two days before you want to eat this delicious bread.

Starter Ingredients

3 medium potatoes

4 cups water

1 Tbsp yeast (or 1 packet)

1 cup warm water

1 cup flour

1/3 cup white sugar

1 and ½ Tbsp salt

Starter Process

Peel and cube potatoes, add to pot with 4 cups of water. Boil for 30 minutes or until soft. Remove from heat. Mash with a potato masher, mixing into the potato water. Cool to room temperature.

Stir in the yeast and warm water. Mix in the flour, sugar, and salt. Cover the bowl with a damp kitchen towel and let sit for 24 hours at room temperature.

Bread Ingredients

1 cup starter

1 and 1/4th cups warm water

1 Tablespoon salt

½ cup sugar

½ cup oil

6 cups flour

Bread Process

In a large bowl add starter, salt, sugar, oil, warm water, and flour. Mix well. If using a standing mixer, add flour until a doughball forms which pulls away from the edge of the bowl and is shiny and elastic. If mixing by hand, add flour and knead the dough until it is shiny and elastic, about ten minutes.

Put oil into a large bowl, roll the dough in the oil, covering the whole surface. Cover the bowl with a damp kitchen towel. Let sit at room temperature for 12 hours.

Punch down dough. Knead on a floured surface to remove bubbles. Form dough into three loaves **or** one loaf and a pan of 16 dinner rolls **or** one loaf and a pan of cinnamon rolls.

Grease the pans, add the shaped dough, cover with a damp towel, and let sit for 6-8 hours.

Once the bread has raised, bake loaves at 350 degrees F for 30 minutes or until a knife inserted in the center comes out clean. Alternately, bake rolls at 375 degrees F. for approximately 20 minutes or until a knife inserted in the center comes out clean.

Sourdough Cinnamon Rolls

Ingredients

2/3rds of a recipe of Rosa's Sourdough Rolls

1 stick butter (softened)

1 cup brown sugar

Cinnamon to taste (cover the sugar in a layer of cinnamon) perhaps 2 Tbsp cinnamon.

Process

Roll out dough on a floured surface into a large rectangle.

Spread softened butter over surface of dough.

Cover in a layer of brown sugar.

Cover in sprinkled cinnamon.

Roll dough up into a log shape.

Cut (either with bread knife or string) into four segments. Cut each segment into either 3 or 4 rounds. Place cinnamon rounds into a greased casserole dish.

Bake at 350 degrees F. for 30 minutes or until a knife inserted in the center comes out clean.

Enjoy with a cup of tea in a fancy teacup!

Kristen Joy Wilks was once a barefoot little girl on horseback, galloping through the remote forests and hidden meadows surrounding a small Bible camp in the Cascade Mountains. She has carried a frog in her pocket, captained dubious watercraft made from old boards and inner tubes, and directed her horse through a herd of 200 elk against all good sense. Due to a brilliant scheme with her cousins, she has even been suspended by her feet over a homemade pit filled with gardener snakes. Despite this experience, she returns to the mountains again and again. Kristen writes from a remote mountain meadow that alternates between quiet and chaos. The mom of three sons, a cat named Whisper Persnickety, and Nessie Grace Karu their giant Newfoundland dog, she lives with her camp director husband at Camas Meadows Bible Camp where she is photographer and camp storyteller. Her stories highlight the humor and grace God gives amidst the detritus of life. Kristen can be found tucked under a tattered quilt at 4:00 a.m. writing a wide variety of implausible tales or at www.kristenjoywilk s.com.

Del and Autumn Griffith with their dog Daisy

ALSO BY KRISTEN JOY WILKS

Books For Readers Ages 6-10

Phooey Kerflooey vs The Fancy, Fancy Teacup

Phooey Kerflooey vs The Battle Squirrel

Phooey Kerflooey vs The Deep, Deep Dark

Books For Readers Ages 9-12

Phooey Kerflooey

The Rough and Rowdy Devotional

Books For Moms and Kids to Read Together

Chicken Crossing (RomCom from a human POV)

Dandelion Floofums (ages 7-11 from a chicken POV)

Books For Teens

The Volk Advent: A Gothic Christmas Mystery

RomComs

Copenhagen Cozenage

Athens Ambuscade

Spider Gap

Yellowstone Yondering

For more information about Kristen's books, please scan below.

To download Kristen's free coloring pages (including Autumn riding the wild burro), please scan below.